HANDY GASTNELL

OPTIONS TRADING

Analyze, Execute, & Reduce Risks to Grow Your Net Worth

BONUS INSIDE

34 TECHNIQUES, TACTICS, & STRATEGIES
to Profit on the Financial Markets
The Ultimate In-Depth Guide for Beginners

© Copyright 2024 - All rights reserved.

The content contained within this book may not be reproduced, duplicated, or transmitted without direct written permission from the author or the publisher.

Under no circumstances will any blame or legal responsibility be held against the publisher or author for any damages, reparation, or monetary loss due to the information contained within this book, either directly or indirectly.

Legal Notice:

This book is copyright-protected. It is only for personal use. You cannot amend, distribute, sell, use, quote, or paraphrase any part of the content within this book without the consent of the author or publisher.

Disclaimer Notice:

Please note that the information contained within this document is for educational and entertainment purposes only. All effort has been executed to present accurate, up-to-date, reliable, and complete information. No warranties of any kind are declared or implied. Readers acknowledge that the author is not engaged in the rendering of legal, financial, medical, or professional advice. The content within this book has been derived from various sources. Please consult a licensed professional before attempting any techniques outlined in this book.

By reading this document, the reader agrees that under no circumstances is the author responsible for any losses, direct or indirect, that are incurred as a result of the use of the information contained within this document, including, but not limited to, errors, omissions, or inaccuracies.

Free Bonuses

Thank you for your purchase! As a token of our appreciation, you now have exclusive access to five invaluable bonuses designed to enhance your understanding of options trading and trading strategies.

Here's a glimpse of what you'll receive:

1. **Trading Strategies: A Concise Guide to Hypothetical Analysis in Options Trading**
2. **Finding Your Edge: A Personal Guide to Assessing Your Options Trading Style**
3. **Quick Wins in Options: The Essential Cheat Sheet for Trading Success**
4. **Test Your Trade: The Technical Readiness Quiz for Options Traders**
5. **Trade and Reflect: The Ultimate Journal Template for Options Traders**

To access these bonuses, simply scan the QR code:

You can also access these valuable resources by visiting https://bit.ly/Gastrell-OT (Attention: The link is case-sensitive. Enter the link exactly as it is, with the correct uppercase and lowercase letters. Otherwise, the link will not work properly).

Support and Feedback

For feedback, questions, or if you encounter any issues, please visit the link or scan the QR code to share your thoughts and get assistance:

https://authorhelpdesk.com/support

Table of Contents

Free Bonuses 3
Support and Feedback 5
Introduction 9
Chapter 1: Introduction to Options Trading 11
    Understanding the Basics 11
    Options Market 12
    The Role of Options in Financial Markets 14
    The History and Evolution 15
    Common Misconceptions and Pitfalls 17
    Evaluating Your Readiness to Trade Options 18
Chapter 2: The Mechanics 25
    Components of Options 25
    Factors Affecting Option Prices 31
    Trading Platforms and Tools 32
    Opening and Closing an Options Trade 37
Chapter 3: Analyzing Options 41
    Fundamental Analysis 41
    Technical Analysis 47
    Sentiment Analysis 52
Chapter 4: Basic Options Trading Strategies 55
    Long Call and Long Put 55
    Covered Call and Protective Put 62
    Bull and Bear Spreads 66

Chapter 5: Advanced Options Trading Strategies 69
Straddles and Strangles 69
Iron Condors and Butterflies 75
Calendar and Diagonal Spreads 79

Chapter 6: Risk Management in Options Trading 83
Understanding and Assessing Risk 83
Risk Management Techniques 87
Diversification 89

Chapter 7: Trading Psychology and Discipline 97
Emotional Challenges in Trading 97
Developing a Trading Plan 101
Maintaining Discipline in Trading 106

Chapter 8: Regulatory and Legal Aspects 111
Regulatory Bodies and Their Roles 111
Legal Considerations 116
Ethical Trading Practices 121

Chapter 9: Building a Successful Career 129
Developing a Consistent Trading Routine 129
Continuous Learning and Adaptation 132
Balancing Trading with Personal Life 134

Conclusion 137

Techniques Recap 139

References 143

Exclusive Bonuses 147

Introduction

Undertaking options trading with zero knowledge will feel like you have slipped into a world of confusion. People often consider it a world filled with confusing charts, unfamiliar terms, and risky choices. With all these aspects, *where will you begin?*

To simplify this complexity, "Options Trading [All in 1]" will sum up the basics of learning options trading. This book will cover all the necessary aspects, including the mechanics of trading, analysis techniques, trading strategies, risk management, trading psychology, and regulatory aspects.

Know how options work, how to buy and sell them, and the essential terminology you need to know. In terms of analysis techniques, there is no need for complex math or confusing algorithms. Instead, this book will show practical ways to evaluate options and make informed decisions. Further deepening your knowledge are the various basic to advanced strategies so you can find the ones that suit your goals.

Of course, no trading journey is complete without understanding risk. "Options Trading [All in 1]" will teach you essential risk management techniques to help you protect your investments. Trading psychology is another essential aspect; delve into the emotional side of trading and provide tips on staying calm under pressure and making rational decisions. Lastly, learn about the rules and regulations governing options trading, ensuring you stay on the right side of the law.

As someone with more than a decade of experience in the financial markets, this book contains 34 techniques, tips, and strategies on options trading peppered throughout the entire book to share these years of knowledge. It is intentionally designed this way to serve as your guide along each step of analyzing the market, developing effective trading strategies, managing risks, and navigating the regulatory landscape.

Whether you are a newbie or just looking to refresh your knowledge, this book will give you a new perspective on options trading in a way that is comprehensive but also practical and accessible. With step-by-step explanations, real-world examples, and practical tips, you can make informed investment decisions. Have the level of flexibility and potential for high returns that are unmatched by other financial instruments.

Get ready to transform the way you think about options trading. No more feeling lost in a sea of technical terms. Say goodbye to confusion and hello to clarity and confidence. Now is the time to make options trading simple, accessible, and profitable.

Chapter 1
Introduction to Options Trading

As you begin your journey into options trading, starting with a solid understanding of the basics is necessary. This chapter will introduce you to the fundamental concepts of options trading, providing a foundation for building your knowledge and skills.

Understanding the Basics

Options trading has its vocabulary because it deals with financial contracts that have specific rules and conditions. Just as learning a new language helps you navigate a foreign country, understanding the language of options trading is vital for making informed decisions and achieving your financial goals.

Starting up, *what exactly are the options?* ***Options*** are financial contracts that give you the right *(but not the obligation)* to buy or sell an underlying asset at a predetermined price ***(the strike price)*** on or before a specific date ***(the expiration date)***. They are like agreements that allow you to decide about buying or selling without committing to it.

Options are often compared to stocks, but they are fundamentally different. When you buy a stock, you own a piece of a company. But with options, you are making a bet on the future price movement of that stock without owning it. This unique characteristic of options sets them apart from traditional stock trading.

There are two types of options: *call options and put options.* A **call option** gives you the right to buy the underlying asset at the strike price, while a **put option** gives you the right to sell it at the strike price. Calls are like a ticket to buy, and puts are like a ticket to sell.

With options, you can create various strategies to profit from different market conditions, even if the market is going up, down, or sideways. The leverage options trading offers allow you to control a substantial amount of the underlying asset with a relatively small investment.

Options Market

Understanding the various participants in options trading and discerning their impact on market prices and activity is integral to mastering the essentials of options trading. This involves acknowledging the roles of:

- **Buyers.** These individuals purchase options to profit based on what they think will happen in the market. For instance, a retail investor might buy call options on tech stocks, anticipating a rise in the sector. Similarly, a hedge fund might buy put options to hedge against potential losses in their portfolio. The volume of options bought can sometimes indicate the prevailing market sentiment.
- **Sellers.** These individuals sell options, often to hedge their positions or earn premium income. For example, a farmer might sell options on their crop to secure a guaranteed price, limiting risk. Institutional investors often sell options as part of complex trading strategies. The dynamics of supply and demand from sellers can significantly influence option prices.

- **Market Makers.** These firms facilitate the smooth functioning of the options market by always offering to buy and sell options. A well-known market maker is Citadel Securities. They profit from the spread between options' buying and selling prices rather than speculating on price movements.
- **Clearinghouses.** These entities act as intermediaries in the options market, ensuring that trading parties adhere to the rules. The *Options Clearing Corporation (OCC)* is a major clearinghouse in the US, overseeing financial transactions and ensuring the integrity of trades.
- **Exchanges.** These are platforms where options are traded. They establish the rules governing the market, including the types of options available and the procedures for trading. The *Chicago Board Options Exchange (CBOE)* is one of the largest, facilitating online trading and offering traders a range of tools and resources.
- **Brokers.** These are individuals or companies that assist everyday investors in trading options. For instance, brokerage firms like Charles Schwab or Robinhood provide platforms where traders can execute options trades, offering various tools and resources to aid decision-making.
- **Regulators.** These government bodies oversee the options market to ensure fairness and safety. In the US, the *Securities and Exchange Commission (SEC)* sets market rules and monitors compliance to protect investors.
- **Data Providers.** These organizations supply traders with information about options, including pricing data and trading volumes. Companies like *Bloomberg* and *Reuters* are renowned for providing comprehensive data that assists traders in making informed decisions.
- **Analysts.** These are experts who analyze the market and offer advice to traders. For instance, *Goldman Sachs* or *Morgan Stanley* analysts often publish research reports predicting market trends, which can influence trading strategies and decisions.

The Role of Options in Financial Markets

In financial markets, options are versatile tools that offer investors and traders opportunities for the following:

- **Risk Management.** Options were created as risk management tools. They provide a means for investors to protect their investments against adverse price movements in the underlying assets. For example:
    - Hedging. Investors can use options to hedge their positions, effectively insuring themselves against potential losses. For instance, stockholders concerned about a market downturn can buy options to limit their downside risk.
- **Speculation.** Options offer speculative opportunities for traders looking to profit from market movements. Traders can take positions based on their expectations of how an asset's price will change. As an example:
    - Call Options. Traders can buy call options if they anticipate the underlying asset's price will rise. This allows them to benefit from price increases without owning the asset outright.
    - Put Options. Traders can purchase put options if they expect the underlying asset's price to fall. This enables them to profit from declining prices.
- **Enhancing Portfolio Returns.** Options can enhance the overall performance of an investment portfolio. Investors can use options strategically to generate income, reduce risk, and optimize returns. For instance:
    - Covered Calls. Investors with long stock positions can sell call options against their holdings to generate additional income through premium collection.
    - Collar Strategies. Investors can use collars, which combine holding a stock, buying protective puts, and

selling covered calls to create a balanced approach that mitigates risk while potentially generating income.
- **Liquidity and Market Efficiency.** Options contribute to the liquidity and efficiency of financial markets. They facilitate price discovery and provide opportunities for market participants to express their views on asset prices, leading to well-functioning markets.
- **Diverse Investment Strategies.** Options offer various investment strategies, from conservative to highly speculative. This diversity allows investors to tailor their approach to risk tolerance and financial goals.

The History and Evolution

As many know it today, options trading is a relatively modern phenomenon. The concept of options, though, has been around for centuries.

Early History

The concept of options trading can be traced back to ancient times. In fact, Aristotle, the famous Greek philosopher, wrote about a story that could be considered the earliest recorded option trade. In his work *"Politics,"* he tells the story of Thales, a poor philosopher from Miletus who used his knowledge of astronomy to predict that the upcoming olive harvest would be particularly bountiful. Thales paid olive press owners a small sum to reserve their presses for the harvest season. When his prediction came true, he could rent the presses at a high price, making a considerable profit. This story, while not an example of options trading in the modern sense, illustrates the basic principle of an option: *paying a small sum to secure the right to buy or sell something later.*

In the 17th century, options were used in the tulip bulb market in Holland. Traders would enter contracts to buy tulip bulbs at a future date for a specified price. However, this market eventually crashed in what is now known as the *"Tulip Mania,"* one of the first recorded speculative bubbles.

Modern Options Trading

The modern era of options trading began in the 20th century. In the early 1900s, *"over-the-counter" (OTC) options* were common in the U.S. These were privately negotiated contracts between two parties. Back then, this market operated with little to no regulation, and trading frequently occurred in *"bucket shops,"* infamous for their vulnerability to fraudulent practices.

The turning point came in 1973 with the establishment of the **Chicago Board Options Exchange (CBOE)**. The CBOE created a standardized and regulated market for options trading, providing a transparent and reliable platform for traders. This was a significant milestone in options trading history, marking the beginning of the modern era of options trading.

In 1973, the **Black-Scholes-Merton model** was also introduced. This mathematical model provided a way to calculate the price of an option, considering factors such as the *price of the underlying asset, the strike price, the time until expiration,* and *the risk-free interest rate.* The model revolutionized options trading, making it more accessible and understandable for traders.

The Impact of Technology

The advent of technology has had a profound impact on options trading. With the rise of the internet in the late 20th century, online trading platforms emerged, providing traders with easy access to financial markets. These platforms allowed anyone with an internet connection to trade options, opening the market to a wider audience.

Technology has also led to the development of sophisticated trading tools and algorithms. These tools can analyze vast amounts of market data in real-time, helping traders make more informed decisions. Algorithms can execute trades at lightning speed, taking advantage of fleeting market opportunities.

Options trading becoming more transparent and efficient is also driven by the technology. Electronic trading platforms provide real-time price quotes, allowing traders to see the current market price of an option at any given time. This transparency helps ensure fair pricing and reduces the likelihood of manipulation.

Common Misconceptions and Pitfalls

Many individuals venturing into options trading often encounter lots of myths and misconceptions. Disposing of these myths is essential to ensure a successful and informed trading experience.

Myths

There is a prevalent notion that trading **options is inherently riskier than trading stocks**. While options can be volatile and speculative, they can also be used as hedging tools to manage and mitigate risk in a portfolio. Contrary to popular belief, options do not just cater to the speculative trader but also to the conservative investor.

Another widespread myth is that **one needs significant capital to start trading options**. In reality, options can often be purchased for a fraction of the cost of the underlying stock, allowing investors with a smaller capital base to participate in stock movements.

Many also believe that **options trading is excessively complicated**. Though it does have its complexities, with proper education and continuous learning, any dedicated individual can grasp its mechanics and strategies.

Common Mistakes to Avoid for Beginners

Beginners entering the options market should be wary of several pitfalls. One of the most common mistakes is ***not having a clear trading plan.*** Setting clear objectives, risk tolerance levels, and exit strategies is necessary before diving into trades.

Many beginners further *fail to diversify their options portfolio*, placing all their capital on a single trade. This approach amplifies the risk. Always spread investments across various assets to cushion against potential losses.

Another mistake to be conscious of is ***ignoring options' intrinsic value and time decay.*** Not considering these factors can result in losses even if the market moves in the predicted direction.

Evaluating Your Readiness to Trade Options

Before diving headfirst into trading options, taking a step back and thoroughly evaluating your readiness is wise. By objectively assessing your motivations, risk appetite, available time, knowledge level, and aptitude before getting started, you can set yourself up for long-term success in options trading.

Initial Assessments

Options trading requires self-awareness and self-understanding. *Figure out what you want to achieve, how much risk you are comfortable with,* and *how much money you can put into trading.*

Understand Your Goals and Motivations

Reflect on why you want to trade options in the first place. Different motivations require different approaches. *Are you looking to use options primarily for hedging purposes to protect your existing investments against adverse price movements? Or is generating additional income through options a major objective?*

Alternatively, *do you plan to trade options more aggressively for speculation, making directional bets on market moves?* Having a clear purpose and aligning your strategies to match is helpful. Those using options mainly for hedging likely require a more conservative strategy with defined risk parameters. Speculative traders, meanwhile, need to be comfortable with inherently higher risks in pursuit of potentially bigger rewards.

Beyond your reasons for trading options, also consider your time horizon. *Are you looking to trade actively, holding positions for shorter durations to capture shorter-term market swings? Or do you have a longer-term focus using options for broad portfolio protection?* Your ideal strategies may vary based on your intended holding period. Defining these motivations and goals is the critical first step.

Gauge Your Risk Tolerance

An honest appraisal of your personal risk tolerance is vital. Trading options come with risk exposures due to inherent leverage. Small price movements in the underlying asset can translate into outsized gains or losses on options contracts. Market volatility can lead to rapid changes in options pricing and portfolio values. *Are you comfortable assuming higher levels of risk? Or do large drawdowns keep you up at night?*

Consider your overall investing philosophy too. *Are you a conservative buy-and-hold investor looking for steady returns? Or an aggressive trader willing to take bigger risks for potentially higher rewards?* Understanding where you fall on this spectrum informs what risk parameters might suit you best. Certain strategies like credit spreads or iron condors may be preferable for those with lower risk tolerance. Aggressive traders might gravitate toward naked options or highly directional exposures.

Gauge your reaction to past investment losses. *How did you cope? Were you able to maintain composure and stick to your plans? Or did anxiety lead you to abandon your strategies prematurely?* Your ability to navigate past drawdowns signals how you might handle the inevitable losses in options trading.

Assess Your Available Capital

Sufficient capital is mandatory to trade options effectively. Unlike stocks, purchasing even one contract requires upfront capital for the options premium. Margin requirements can also be substantial for certain strategies. Aim to start trading options only when you have adequate capital available beyond other financial needs.

A prudent rule of thumb is limiting your risk on any options trade to 1% to 2% of your capital allocated to options trading. For a $10,000 account, risk no more than $100 to $200 per trade. Doing so ensures a string of losses does not wipe out your entire capital.

When starting, only allocate capital you can afford to lose and treat options trading as an educational expense. Avoid funding accounts through loans or credit cards. Remember that even skilled traders face losses. Size your trading suitably for your available capital rather than seeking windfalls on single trades.

Gearing Up for Trading

After knowing your trading preferences, learn and prepare yourself. This step is essential because it forms the foundation for your trading journey.

Build Your Knowledge Foundation

Before trading options, build foundational knowledge through books, online courses, and demo trading accounts. Understand factors influencing options pricing, risk graphs of basic strategies, order types, and technical analysis basics.

Paper trade options contracts for several months to reinforce theoretical knowledge with practical experience. Paper trading allows you to simulate live trading in real market conditions without risking actual capital. The lessons learned can be invaluable before committing real dollars.

While acquiring knowledge is ongoing, ensure you have a baseline before starting. Trading without understanding options sensitivities or how pricing works invites potential disasters. Feel confident in comprehending market dynamics and probabilistic outcomes for different options strategies.

Develop Your Emotional Discipline

Trading requires rationally executing your strategies, unclouded by fear or greed. But, allowing emotions to override your planned decisions is common among new traders. Fear can lead to premature exits from trades even when the original reasoning behind the trade remains valid. Greed can further tempt you to hold onto substantial gains, only to watch those profits vanish when you fail to adhere to your exit rules.

Before attempting live trading, assess your ability to stick to plans during stressful moments. Practicing with demo trading can help uncover and address psychological vulnerabilities. *Can you consistently follow stop-loss orders even after experiencing several losing trades?* If you have set a profit target, *do you possess the discipline to take profits once that target is reached?* Trading psychology is a skill that must be honed over time through practical experience. Never underestimate emotions' significant role in undermining otherwise well-constructed trading strategies.

Now that you know your own trading preferences, it's time to learn and prepare yourself. This step is important because it forms the foundation for your trading journey. This is where you'll really grow your understanding and get ready to make smart decisions in the trading world.

Getting Involved with the Markets

As you enter trading, stay eager to learn and adapt. Explore effective time management, find valuable resources and communities, and gradually apply your knowledge in actual trading situations.

Evaluate Your Available Time

Succeeding in options trading requires substantial time commitment. Analyzing potential trades, monitoring open positions, staying up-to-date on market news, and managing trades requires dedicating significant time each week. For active traders, the time inputs can resemble a full-time job.

Take an honest look at your schedule. Factor in your work, family, and other commitments. *Do you have at least 10 to 15 hours weekly to commit to options trading-related activities? Can you dedicate focused time during normal market hours?* For part-time options traders, reasonable expectations are key. Carve out pockets of time when you can be consistent rather than sporadic.

The effort and time required can also fluctuate based on market conditions. During high-volatility periods, positions may require closer monitoring and rapid adjustments. Even slower market environments still necessitate regular analysis and planning. Incorporate time for expanding your trading knowledge through reading, courses, and practice too. Evaluate if you can allot the requisite time inputs for your goals.

Seek Educational Resources and Communities

When starting out, obtaining guidance from experienced options traders can substantially shorten your learning curve. Seek out trusted options trading coaches, join online or local trading groups to connect with like-minded individuals, and follow along with reputable traders on platforms like Twitter and YouTube.

An ideal mentor trades profitably over the long term, teaches proven strategies, emphasizes risk management, and takes a systematic, probability-based approach to markets. Beware of flashy market gurus promising get-rich-quick systems. Absorb the wisdom of seasoned mentors but ultimately craft strategies aligned with your risk tolerances.

Surrounding yourself with experienced options traders gives you a support group to rely on during challenging times. You can gain reassurance in your approach while learning new perspectives. Mentors can also provide guidance when you face dilemmas, helping you avoid costly mistakes early on.

Put Knowledge Into Practice Gradually

Take an incremental approach when trading options and begin trading live with small position sizes. This allows you to gain experience reading price action, gauging volatility, managing trades, and controlling emotions while limiting financial risks. Options trading presents an unrelenting learning curve, and starting small avoids being overwhelmed.

Before placing real trades, begin by paper trading for several months to solidify your knowledge, strategies, and risk management rules. Then, transition to single-contract trades while closely tracking trading metrics like profit factor and win rate. Increase position sizes slowly as your strategy is refined and profitability improves over multiple months. Patience starting pays off long-term.

Beware of early large wins also, as these can provide a false sense of trading aptitude before experience is truly gained. Sustainable success requires surviving and overcoming inevitable drawdowns rather than capitalizing on a few outsized gainers early on. Grow your account steadily in sync with your knowledge.

Mastering the mental game, risk control, and emotions are integral skills alongside options theory. But with prudent preparation, perseverance, and an incremental approach, trading options can be fulfilling with strong profit potential. Those who respect the learning curve and evolution must trade consistently while curbing risk and position themselves to reap the advantages and opportunities markets offer over the long haul.

Chapter 2
The Mechanics

For prospective traders and keen market participants, understanding how options operate is not just a prerequisite but a continual learning process that molds your ability to leverage these instruments effectively.

In this chapter, delve deeper into the mechanics of options trading, exploring its various components and functionalities. It will demystify the essential elements of options and illustrate how a solid grasp of them is vital in crafting strategic trading decisions, optimizing risk management, and realizing potential opportunities in the dynamic financial markets.

Components of Options

Different options trading elements are vital for beginner and experienced traders, including the following:

Call Options

Through the mechanisms of call options require a comprehension of the inherent rights and obligations associated with them. These are instrumental in formulating strategies and managing risks effectively in the unpredictable world of options trading.

Rights of Call Option Buyers

Buyers are propelled by the aspiration to leverage market movements, and their journey in this dynamic environment is marked by specific rights that serve as guiding lights amid the ebbs and flows of market valuations.

- **Right to Buy.** This right is executed at any time before the expiration for American-style options and at the expiration for European-style options.
- **Limited Loss.** The buyer's loss is capped at the premium paid, ensuring limited risk regardless of the underlying asset's price variations.

Obligations of Call Option Sellers

The sellers, or writers, undertake a meticulous journey of balancing risks and rewards. They navigate through market dynamics, where the profit potential is juxtaposed with substantial risk, necessitating a thorough understanding of their obligatory landscape.

- **Obligation to Sell.** Upon the exercise of a call option, sellers are bound to deliver the underlying asset at the strike price. This obligation can lead to losses if the market price is substantially higher than the strike price at delivery time.
- **Unlimited Loss Potential.** Sellers face the prospect of infinite losses due to the potential unlimited rise in the underlying asset's price, especially when the option is uncovered or naked.
- **Premium as Income.** The initial premium paid by the buyer serves as an income for the seller, offering some compensation for the associated risks.

Put Options

Put options hold a unique position, allowing investors to navigate through diverse market conditions and fostering strategies that can thrive in various environments. Understanding the rights and obligations associated with put options to utilize them effectively.

Rights of the Put Option Buyer

When an investor buys a put option, they acquire the right that provides them with a safety net, allowing them to profit from a decline in the asset's value or to hedge against potential losses in other investments.

- **Potential Profit.** The buyer can earn profits if the underlying asset's price falls below the strike price, allowing them to sell the asset at a higher price than the current market value.
- **Hedge and Protection.** Investors often use put options as insurance to protect the value of their holdings in the underlying asset against adverse price movements.
- **Leverage.** The buyer can gain exposure to the underlying asset's price movements with a relatively small capital outlay *(the premium paid)*.

Obligations of the Put Option Seller

The seller of a put option is obligated to buy the underlying asset from the put buyer at the strike price if the buyer decides to exercise the option. The seller receives the premium from the buyer as compensation for taking on this risk.

- **Compulsory Purchase.** If the put buyer exercises the option, the put seller must purchase the underlying asset

at the agreed-upon strike price, potentially at a higher cost than the current market price.
- **Premium Income.** The seller earns the premium, providing an immediate inflow of funds. This income can be retained as profit if the option expires unexercised or can offset losses incurred if the option is exercised.
- **Risk Exposure.** The risk for the put seller is significant, as they may be required to buy the underlying asset at a price considerably higher than its current market value. The premium received somewhat mitigates this risk, but losses can still be substantial.

Strike Price

The relationship between the strike price and the current market price of the underlying asset is vital in determining the intrinsic value of an option and its premium.

In scenarios where the underlying asset's market price is above the strike price for a call option, the option is said to be *"in-the-money."* For a put option, it is in-the-money when the underlying asset's market price is below the strike price. In-the-money options have intrinsic value, whereas those *"out-of-the-money"* *(market price is below the strike price for calls, above for puts)* do not.

The strike price is significant because it is a key determinant of whether exercising the option will benefit the holder. The strike price selection is a strategic decision traders make based on their market outlook, risk tolerance, and investment objectives. For example, options with a strike price far from the current market price might be less expensive but are also more risky as the underlying asset price has to move significantly for the option to become profitable.

Expiration Date

Once an option expires, it becomes void, and the holder loses the right to buy or sell the underlying asset at the strike price.

The time until expiration is essential because it impacts the time value component of the option's premium. Options with longer expiration are generally more expensive as they provide the underlying asset more time to move favorably for the option holder. This time allows for the possibility of the option being in-the-money at expiration, and it is also associated with the level of uncertainty and risk in options pricing.

Time decay is a phenomenon associated with the expiration date, representing the rate at which the option loses value as it approaches its expiration. Time decay accelerates as the option gets closer to its expiration date, particularly affecting the premium of the option. This is especially significant for options traders who do not intend to exercise the option but aim to profit from selling the option at a higher premium.

Premium

The premium in options trading is often viewed as the price an investor pays for the option. When an investor buys an option, be it a call or a put, the seller pays the premium. This premium is influenced by multiple factors: *the present price of the underlying asset, the strike price, the remaining time until expiration, the underlying asset's volatility,* and *prevailing market interest rates.*

Two primary components compromise a premium: *intrinsic value and time value.* **Intrinsic value** is the tangible value of the option if exercised at a given time. For example, with a stock trading at $55 and a call option with a strike price of $50, the intrinsic value stands at $5. In contrast, ***time value*** reflects the option's potential future value based on its remaining lifespan. As the expiration date approaches, this time value diminishes, a process termed time decay.

Note that the premium does not remain constant. Changes in the factors above can lead to fluctuations in the premium. A movement in the underlying asset's price towards the option's strike price can amplify the premium. As the option nears its expiration, its premium also often drops due to the dwindling time value.

Option Contracts & Lot Size

An **option contract** denotes a standardized amount of the underlying asset. In purchasing or selling an option, an investor does not deal with a single unit or share of the underlying asset but rather with a set amount delineated by that option contract. Such standardization is vital as it sustains the liquidity of the options market, ensuring a robust presence of buyers and sellers.

Lot size defines the quantity of the underlying asset controlled by one option contract. A standard lot size for numerous stock options is 100 shares. Purchasing a single-call option contract on a stock grants control over 100 shares of that stock until the option reaches its expiration. If an investor chooses to exercise the option, it means buying or selling the 100 shares at the option contract's specified strike price.

The lot size, however, is not universally constant for all options. While 100 shares may be the norm for several stock options, index or futures options may have varied lot sizes. Recognizing the exact lot size for a specific option is essential to gauge potential exposure accurately.

Understand also the multiplier effect of the option contract. Given that an option contract often covers multiple units of the underlying asset, even minor price shifts in the asset can lead to notable profit or loss. As an illustration, with a call option on a stock with a lot size of 100 shares, a mere $1 increment in the stock price can result in a prospective profit of $100, excluding the paid premium.

Factors Affecting Option Prices

Several elements influence option pricing beyond the primary determinants, such as:

- **Dividends.** Stocks that pay dividends can impact option prices, especially if dividends are expected before an option's expiration. When a company announces a dividend, the value of call options may decrease as the stock price typically drops by the dividend amount on the ex-dividend date. In contrast, the value of put options may increase.
- **Supply and Demand.** The forces of supply and demand also influence option prices. A high demand for a specific option contract can increase its premium, irrespective of other static determinants.
- **Market Sentiments.** The sentiment of market participants influences option prices. General optimism about a stock or sector can lead to a rise in call option prices, while pessimism or market downturns can elevate the value of put options.
- **Political and Economic Events.** Whether domestic or international, events that introduce significant market volatility can alter option pricing. Factors such as elections, geopolitical tensions, decisions by central banks, or significant policy announcements can shift option prices as traders adjust their expectations.
- **Corporate Actions.** Certain actions by a company, like stock splits, mergers, or acquisitions, can affect the stock's price and, consequently, its related option prices. For

instance, a stock split can alter the number of shares a trader controls, affecting the option's intrinsic value.
- **Liquidity.** Options traded frequently often have narrow bid-ask spreads. Illiquid options, meanwhile, may have broader spreads, which can influence the prices at which positions are entered or exited.
- **Brokerage Fees.** Though not part of the option's intrinsic or extrinsic value, fees linked with buying and selling options can affect trade profitability, shaping a trader's view of an option's value.

As market conditions shift and evolve, these secondary factors can emerge as main influencers, highlighting their significance in options trading.

Trading Platforms and Tools

Many different computer programs and tool choices exist for people wanting to trade. *Trading tools* comprise software applications or features crafted to aid traders in diverse trading facets, from market analysis to strategy formulation and adept trade execution.

Charting tools are foundational for traders, facilitating the graphical representation of market data through diverse chart types such as line charts, bar charts, and candlestick charts. By leveraging these charts, you gain insights into market trends, distinctive patterns, and potential market pivot points. Advanced versions of these tools further enrich analysis by offering functionalities like *trendline drawing capabilities, Fibonacci retracement plotting,* and the *integration of multiple analytical indicators.*

Trading in options involves a fair amount of calculations. *Options calculators,* tailored for this specialization, empower you to compute potential profits, gauge potential losses, and assess risks linked with myriad options strategies. These calculators adeptly determine intrinsic value, time value, and even the elusive implied volatility of options. They fortify decision-making capabilities by providing a clearer understanding of the option's value. Some advanced calculators further enhance decision-making by facilitating scenario analysis, enabling traders to manipulate variables like asset price, inherent volatility, and time to envisage the resultant effects on option values.

Real-time market data is also indispensable for traders, delivering instantaneous insights into prevailing market conditions. This includes vital data such as precise price quotes, comprehensive volume data, and timely news dispatches. Such real-time information is pivotal, as even minuscule delays can critically alter trade profitability. Certain advanced trading platforms extend the utility by offering streaming market data, ensuring traders remain abreast of market fluctuations without interruption.

Analytical tools provide a lens through which traders assess market conditions and craft strategies. These encompass technical analysis tools for historical price movement scrutiny and pattern identification. They also include fundamental analysis tools to evaluate a company's inherent financial stability thoroughly. For those navigating the options market, specialized tools such as *volatility charts* and *probability calculators* guide traders in assessing probable outcomes aligned with various options strategies.

Simulators, often called *paper trading tools,* present traders with a platform to refine their trading acumen using virtual currency. By creating a risk-averse environment, these tools permit you to amass experience, validate strategies, and deeply understand options market intricacies. Such platforms are instrumental in fostering confidence and establishing a firm foundation for traders, setting the stage for their eventual foray into live trading environments where real capital is at stake.

Things to Consider When Choosing a Trading Platform

Given the multitude of platforms, an informed decision becomes imperative. Here are relevant factors for consideration:

- **User Interface and Experience.** Platforms with intuitive design and straightforward navigation foster better trading activities. Platforms should offer clear font choices, responsive design, and easy access to essential tools, especially during swift market movements.
- **Available Tools and Features.** Modern trading platforms are packed with tools for technical analysis, trend prediction, and market research. Platforms should offer charting tools, historical data access, real-time price tracking, and automated trading features.
- **Security and Encryption.** Security remains a priority, especially with sensitive financial data and funds at stake. Platforms must implement strong encryption, two-factor authentication, and stringent security protocols.
- **Costs and Fees.** Platforms differ in their fee structures. Some charge per trade, while others operate on monthly subscription fees. Understanding these costs helps in financial planning and prevents unforeseen charges. Hidden fees, including withdrawal or inactivity fees, should also be scrutinized.
- **Customer Support and Service.** Traders, regardless of their experience, may face technical challenges. Platforms with swift, knowledgeable customer support are invaluable. Multiple communication avenues should be available, such as chat, email, and phone support.
- **Platform Reliability and Uptime.** Continuous accessibility to financial markets is paramount. Chosen platforms must guarantee high reliability and uptime. Downtime or glitches can be detrimental, leading to potential losses or missed opportunities.

- **Customizability and Personalization.** Traders possess individualized strategies and preferences. Platforms that permit users to tailor layouts, tools, and settings enhance the trading experience.
- **Educational Resources.** For those new to trading, platforms equipped with educational resources are advantageous. These resources encompass webinars, tutorials, articles, and demo accounts.
- **Supported Assets and Markets.** Traders should ensure platforms support their trading interests, whether stocks, forex, commodities, or cryptocurrencies.
- **Mobile and Desktop Accessibility.** The contemporary trading landscape requires platforms to be accessible across devices. Platforms that are available on both desktop and mobile versions are pivotal.
- **Integration with Other Tools.** Traders utilizing third-party tools for analysis or strategies should prefer platforms that integrate effortlessly with these tools.
- **Community and Social Trading Features.** Some platforms house community forums or social trading avenues. These enable traders to share insights and serve as a resource hub for newcomers and veterans.
- **Regulation and Licensing.** Platforms operating under esteemed regulatory bodies offer enhanced trust and security. Opting for platforms transparent about their licenses and regulatory adherence is recommended.

The Importance of a Reliable Internet Connection

Daily activities, including financial transactions, have migrated online in today's digital age. The domain of options trading, a segment of the financial world, is no exception due to the following reasons:

- **Timely Execution of Trades.** Options trading operates in a dynamic environment where asset prices fluctuate frequently. To capitalize on favorable market conditions or minimize potential losses, traders must execute trades promptly. A lagging or interrupted internet connection can lead to missed opportunities or unfavorable trade executions. In worst-case scenarios, a delay of even a few seconds can translate into substantial financial setbacks.

- **Access to Real-Time Market Data.** Making informed trading decisions necessitates access to real-time market data. Traders rely on up-to-the-second information on stock prices, market trends, news updates, and other pertinent data. An inconsistent internet connection might mean receiving outdated information, jeopardizing decision-making and strategic planning.
- **Smooth Operation of Trading Platforms.** Most options traders employ specialized software platforms for analysis, charting, and trade execution. While offering advanced functionalities, these platforms require a stable internet connection to function seamlessly. Any disruptions can hinder the platform's performance, obstructing a trader's workflow and analytical processes.
- **Security Concerns.** Financial transactions demand top-tier security. Disruptions or inconsistencies in an internet connection can pose risks. For instance, if a connection drops midway through a transaction, it might leave the trader uncertain about their trade status. Repeated disconnections can make a trader's system vulnerable to security breaches or cyber-attacks.
- **Continuous Learning and Updates.** The world of options trading is vast, and continuous learning is integral to a trader's success. Webinars, online courses, and financial news streams are essential resources that traders use to stay updated. A reliable internet connection ensures uninterrupted access to these educational materials, allowing traders to keep abreast of the latest strategies, market news, and updates.

- **Collaboration and Communication.** Often, traders collaborate with peers, mentors, or teams to discuss strategies, seek advice, or share insights. Platforms like Zoom, Skype, or proprietary trading communication tools have become the norm. A stable internet connection ensures clear and uninterrupted communication, fostering effective collaboration.
- **Backup and Cloud Storage.** Many traders back up their trading strategies, historical data, and other crucial information on the cloud. Regular backups reduce the risk of data loss due to hardware failures. A steady and fast internet connection is vital to efficiently save and retrieve data from cloud storage.

While the intricacies of options trading revolve around understanding market dynamics, strategies, and financial instruments, a reliable internet connection supports all these activities.

Opening and Closing an Options Trade

Trading options is a dynamic process that involves several steps, such as:

Placing an Order

Engaging in options trading necessitates the initiation of an order. This initial step requires a trader to select the precise option they wish to engage with, either a call or a put. Determine the strike price and the expiration date, alongside the decision to buy or sell the option.

During the order process, there is a need to designate the order's nature: *market or limit*. **Market orders** seek execution at the most favorable current market price. **Limit orders,** meanwhile, only see execution at a designated price or one even better. Grasping the nuances between these order types is necessary, as their strategic deployment hinges on the prevailing market conditions and the trader's strategy.

Beyond these foundational order elements, find the need to integrate further conditions into your order, such as stop or trailing stop orders. These specific order types aim to trim potential losses or solidify gains. While they offer substantial advantages in risk management, a comprehensive understanding of their operational dynamics and optimal deployment timing is necessary.

Monitoring a Trade

Following the successful placement and execution of an order, diligent trade monitoring becomes paramount. This task encompasses observing the price behavior of the underlying asset, fluctuations in the option's price, and other pivotal factors with the potential to alter the trade's trajectory.

Trade monitoring surpasses mere price observations. A sharp trader remains vigilant of relevant market news and events with potential ramifications for the underlying asset. Events like corporate earnings disclosures, releases of macroeconomic indicators, and shifts in overall market sentiment can drastically influence an option's valuation.

Aside from these external market factors, self-assessment and introspection are integral to trade monitoring. A trader must maintain a meticulous record of their trading outcomes, both successes and setbacks. Such records facilitate introspective analysis, allowing traders to evaluate their decisions, rectify missteps, and strengthen their trading understanding over time.

Closing a Trade

The act of closing a trade carries significance that goes beyond a mere transaction. The proper management of liquidity risk stands critical for traders during this process. ***Liquidity*** delineates the ease with which an options contract can be sold or purchased without causing drastic shifts in its price. Notably, options with broader bid-ask spreads or lower trading volumes bear heightened liquidity risk.

When contemplating exiting positions, traders study the liquidity attributes of their specific options contracts. It is observed that options, especially those actively traded and falling within the front-month and at-the-money category, usually display the most compact bid-ask spreads. In contrast, options with longer expiration durations or deep in or out of the money often manifest expansive spreads.

A cautious approach for traders involves the ***segmentation of the closing transactions.*** Instead of attempting to exit a trade in its entirety instantaneously, dividing it into smaller segments for closure over time can prove advantageous. In scenarios where options are not very liquid, introducing a substantial order immediately might inadvertently create unfavorable market movements against the position. Gradual exits or *"legging out"* of trades in smaller portions allow traders to navigate liquidity challenges adeptly.

In instances where market dynamics are unfavorable and rapidly moving against prevailing open positions, you should exercise caution. ***Resist impulsive actions***, such as quickly selling or buying market-price options to terminate the trade. Such haste can culminate in undesirable order completions, especially in volatile market conditions. A more calculated approach entails the *utilization of limit orders, patiently awaiting improved entry* or *exit pricing opportunities.*

For those options that are markedly illiquid, an alternative strategy emerges. ***Employ the underlying asset,*** be it a stock or an ETF, to conclude their positions. This involves executing transactions in the underlying entity to counterbalance the directional implications stemming from the options contracts.

The direct mechanics of closing a trade in the options domain demand thoughtful management in practice. By critically evaluating liquidity circumstances, modulating trade sizes, and opting for judicious order varieties, you can ensure effective and efficient exit strategies.

Chapter 3
Analyzing Options

Unraveling the complexities of options trading requires a keen understanding of fundamental, technical, and sentiment analysis. This chapter delves into these key areas, exploring the impact of financial statements, economic indicators, and corporate news on options prices. It further illuminates the role of chart patterns, technical indicators, and volume and opens interest in technical analysis. Lastly, it sheds light on the importance of market sentiment and psychology in options trading.

Fundamental Analysis

Fundamental analysis is a method of evaluating security to measure its intrinsic value by examining related economic and financial factors. This includes *macroeconomic factors*, such as the state of the economy and industry conditions, and *microeconomic factors*, like the effectiveness of the company's management. The goal is to determine a number that an investor can compare with a security's current price to see whether the security is undervalued or overvalued.

Understanding Financial Statements

Financial statements provide a detailed picture of a company's financial health, performance, and value. By knowing how to read and interpret these statements, you can make informed decisions about the intrinsic value of an option's underlying asset. The three most critical financial statements are the *balance sheet, income statement, and cash flow statement.*

Balance Sheet

The balance sheet is a fundamental financial statement, encapsulating a company's financial standing at a particular moment. It enumerates the company's assets, liabilities, and the equity shareholders hold. This financial tool serves multiple purposes: *it gauges the financial robustness of a company, pinpoints avenues for growth, determines the company's risk threshold,* and *contributes to the precision of options pricing.*

Within options pricing, a balance sheet often correlates with reduced implied volatility, a metric that reflects anticipated future fluctuations of the underlying asset.

A fortified balance sheet signifies a company's capability to honor its financial commitments, even in scenarios where the underlying asset's price sees considerable reductions. The confidence investors place in such companies reduces the necessity for a hefty premium when the option of selling the underlying asset arises, leading to a contraction in implied volatility.

To illustrate, consider a scenario where an individual contemplates acquiring a call option linked to a company's stock boasting a substantial balance sheet. The inherent implied volatility associated with this call option would likely be more restrained than an option connected to a company's stock with a more precarious financial stance. This dynamic emerges because sellers of the call option, in this context, carry fewer apprehensions regarding the company's potential to default on financial commitments.

Income Statement

The income statement, often termed the ***profit and loss statement,*** presents a detailed overview of a company's financial performance, encapsulating its revenues, costs, and expenses within a designated timeframe. It begins by listing the total revenue or sales of the company. From this, the cost of goods sold is subtracted, resulting in the gross profit. To determine the net income, which represents the company's earnings following all deductions, further subtractions are made for operating expenses, interest, and taxes.

For individuals involved in options trading, the income statement gauges a company's financial health and its trajectory in terms of profitability. Observing and analyzing the net income trends can offer predictive insights. For instance, companies that consistently report an upward trend in net income are likely to witness an appreciation in their stock prices. This positive momentum may lead to a bullish sentiment, raising the price of call options. When a company reports a consistent decline in net income, it can be a sign of underlying issues, leading to a downward movement in its stock price. This downturn could result in a bearish sentiment in the market, influencing the price of put options negatively.

The income statement further assists options traders in assessing other key performance indicators, such as profit margins or *earnings before interest and taxes (EBIT)*. These metrics can offer deeper insights into a company's operational efficiency and ability to generate profits before external financial obligations. Such insights can further shape the strategies traders adopt in the options market.

Cash Flow Statement

The cash flow statement is a financial document shedding light on a company's cash generated and expended within a specified timeframe. It organizes these flows into three distinct sections:

- **Operating activities.** Outline cash flows stemming from the primary business functions of the company. These encompass cash obtained from sales, funds gathered from

the liquidation of inventory, and cash amassed through the collection of accounts receivable.
- **Investing activities.** Encapsulate cash flows that originate from transactions related to long-term assets. Purchasing or disposing of assets like property, plant, and equipment fall under this category. Such activities cover cash inflow from offloading investments and **proceeds from offering loans to other entities.**
- **Financing activities.** Focus on cash flows linked to a company's capital structure. They encompass cash inflow from securing new debt or issuing stock and outflow from debt repayment, stock repurchases, and dividend disbursements.

For options traders, the cash flow statement proves invaluable. It offers profound insights into the company's fiscal robustness and forward-looking potential. A firm amassing substantial cash from its operations often indicates stability and diminished risk. Such companies, exuding robust operational cash flow, often witness reduced implied volatility—a favorable scenario for those traders keen on option selling.

Economic Indicators

Economic indicators serve as statistical metrics instrumental in analyzing current market conditions or foreseeing potential market trajectories. They offer deep insights into the vitality of an economy and wield influence over financial markets, including the domain of options trading. Such indicators include the following:

- **Consumer Price Index (CPI).** CPI stands as a meter for inflation. It encapsulates consumers' average periodic price alterations for various goods and services. A surge in inflation may instigate central banks to amplify interest rates, aiming to tether soaring inflation and directing

heightened market volatility. Such fluctuations can augment options prices since options often command higher prices in rough markets. Subdued inflation might pave the way for reduced interest rates, diminishing market volatility and the value of options.
- **Gross Domestic Product (GDP) Growth.** GDP growth offers a comprehensive snapshot of economic dynamism within a nation's borders. It explains if an economy is on an expansionary trajectory or experiencing contraction. Strong GDP growth often resonates with a resilient economy, fostering optimistic market perspectives and influencing the valuation of call options. Negative GDP growth can indicate economic deceleration or even a full-blown recession, casting shadows of pessimism over market scenarios affecting the valuation of put options.
- **Interest Rates.** A nation's central banking apparatus determines interest rates and imprints on financial landscapes. Elevated interest rates amplify borrowing expenses, restraining economic expansion and heralding pessimistic market moods. Such environments can bolster the allure of put options, elevating their valuation. In juxtaposition, diminished interest rates reduce borrowing overheads, igniting economic expansion and optimistic market moods. These climates can stress call options, pushing their valuations upwards.

Delving beyond these expansive economic indicators, intricate, sector-specific determinants can shape the contours of options trading. For instance, for individuals venturing into options trading linked to a technology entity's shares, indicators such as technological sector expansion, technological investment thresholds, and shifts in technological consumer patterns become vital.

- **Sector Growth.** An accelerated expansion within a sector can guide optimistic market climates for stocks affiliated with that sector, boosting the valuation of associated call options. The deceleration in sectoral growth might usher in pessimistic market climates, possibly elevating the valuation of put options.

- **Levels of Technological Investment.** Substantial investment influx often signifies a buoyant sentiment towards the technological arena, fostering optimistic market climates. In contrast, a light investment landscape might indicate diminished confidence, potentially shaping pessimistic market climates.
- **Trends in Technological Consumer Behavior.** Evolving consumer patterns can mold the fortunes of technology-centric enterprises. For instance, a surge in the adoption rate of a novel technology can create optimistic market scenarios for entities operating within that niche. A waning consumer interest might direct pessimistic market climates.

The Impact of Corporate News on Options Prices

Corporate news encompasses a vast array of information pertinent to a particular corporation. This news sphere encapsulates earnings reports, managerial shifts, product introductions, collaborative ventures such as mergers or acquisitions, and many other events. Such information influences a company's stock value and the valuation of options linked to that stock.

Earnings reports, which corporations periodically release, offer an insightful gaze into a company's financial health. These declarations, especially when they depict financial outcomes surpassing market anticipations, can act as catalysts, driving the company's stock price upwards. In such scenarios, the valuation of call options, signifying the prerogative to purchase the stock, may surge.

Conversely, the value of put options, representing the entitlement to offload the stock, might decline.

Announcements, such as managerial reconfigurations within a corporation, might create ambiguity regarding the enterprise's future trajectory. Such scenarios can augment the volatility associated with the company's stock. Amplified volatility often translates to heightened option premiums, rendering the options more expensive.

Corporate disclosures further carry the potential to alter the implied volatility linked with options. Should a company disseminate information hinting at potential augmented volatility in its stock, the ensuing aftermath might be a spike in the implied volatility of associated options, leading to an elevation in its valuation.

For an options trader, continuous vigilance over corporate news, comprehension of its implications, and strategic assimilation of such insights into trading decisions are indispensable. This necessitates regular monitoring of press releases, earnings announcements, and other conduits broadcasting corporate news. A deep-rooted understanding of the diverse ramifications each news type might have on option prices remains essential.

Technical Analysis

Technical analysis delves into examining historical market data, emphasizing the intricacies of the supply-and-demand equilibrium as manifested through stock prices. One of the remarkable attributes of technical analysis is its capability to visually represent changes in supply and demand, evident in various chart patterns. This form of analysis encompasses the emotional dimensions of the market, recognizing that human sentiment and psychology play roles in price movements.

Chart Patterns and Trend Analysis

Chart patterns and trend analysis serve as pillars in technical analysis. These visual cues offer insights into market dynamics, aiding in discerning underlying trends and facilitating educated forecasts regarding prospective price trajectories.

Trends

At its essence, a trend embodies the prevailing trajectory of a market or an asset's price spanning a specific duration. Complementing this, a trend line pinpoints and harnesses such directional momentum. The start of trends emerges from the complex interplay between buyers and sellers. Their persistence stems from their propensity to sustain their direction. The fractal nature of trends further implies their manifestation across varied time spans while retaining consistent behavioral patterns. Trends surpass mere algorithmic constructs and resist simplistic computational simulations, given that influences from shorter and longer adjacent trends further complicate their intricacies.

Broadly, trends can be classified into *uptrends, downtrends, or sideways trends:*

- **Uptrends.** These trends exhibit a pattern of escalating highs and lows. The continual establishment of new high and low price points underscores the dominant buying sentiment, overpowering the selling thrust.
- **Downtrends.** Marked by diminishing highs and lows, downtrends signal a prevailing selling sentiment, overshadowing buying impulses. The price of the concerned asset consistently realizes newer low points, painting a scenario of descending price momentum.

- **Sideways Trends.** The asset's price fluctuates within a confined spectrum, suggesting an equilibrium between buying and selling forces, leading to an absence of a definitive trend direction.

Trends possess variable lifespans, ranging from transient phases spanning mere days to more enduring ones extending across years. Typically, the longevity of a trend is directly proportional to its propensity to persist. However, the volatile nature of markets means that trends remain susceptible to reversals irrespective of their strength or duration. Exercise caution, continually monitoring market conditions to mitigate potential adversities while capitalizing on trend-driven opportunities.

Support and Resistance

Two pivotal pillars in trend analysis are support and resistance. The concept of *support* can be visualized as a horizontal boundary, drawn connecting multiple troughs that share a consistent price level. *Resistance* represents a similar horizontal demarcation, connecting peaks at a consistent price level. The strongness of these levels varies, primarily influenced by the timeframes they are extrapolated from.

Moving Averages

Moving averages, often abbreviated as MAs, discern a trend's onset, continuation, or potential reversal. By allocating equivalent weightage to each time frame, MAs facilitate the recognition of trends. A scenario where a sensitive or fast *Simple Moving Average (SMA)* surpasses a less sensitive or slow SMA from beneath is interpreted as a bullish sign. When the fast SMA descends below the slow SMA, it signals a bearish trend.

Breakouts

A breakout manifests when a price transcends defined boundaries, be it a trend line, support, resistance level, or zone, either upward or downward. While trend line breakouts often herald the culmination of a trend, surpassing support or resistance levels typically indicates the inception of a new trend. Numerous trading systems that boast success leverage breakout strategies as their foundation.

Bollinger Bands

Bollinger Bands, conceptualized as price envelopes, are drafted at standard deviation levels above and below an SMA of the price. These bands offer insights into whether the prices of assets are inflated or deflated relative to their historical averages. When the bands constrict, it indicates a period of subdued volatility. Such constriction often precedes significant price movements in either trajectory.

Technical Indicators and Oscillators

Technical indicators and oscillators are heuristic or pattern-based signals produced by the price, volume, and open interest of a security or contract. By analyzing historical data, these indicators can help predict future price movements. Some of the common technical indicators include the *Relative Strength Index (RSI), Money Flow Index (MFI), stochastics, moving average convergence divergence (MACD),* and *Bollinger Bands.*

There are two categories under technical indicators: *overlays and oscillators.* **Overlays** are technical indicators that use the same scale as prices and are plotted over the top of the prices on a stock chart. Examples include *moving averages* and *Bollinger Bands.* **Oscillators**, on the other hand, oscillate between a local minimum and maximum and are plotted above or below a price chart, such as the *stochastic oscillator, MACD,* or *RSI*.

These indicators are not just for active traders. Even long-term investors can use technical indicators to identify entry and exit points.

Volume and Open Interest Analysis

Volume quantifies the number of contracts transacted over a specified time frame. This metric is pivotal in understanding the current level of trader activity in a particular option. When volume is elevated, it suggests a pronounced activity level, often accompanying significant price shifts. A diminished volume, meanwhile, might imply a neutral interest in a particular price direction. The volume further plays a role in verifying trends. An upward price movement with surging volume typically sends a strong, bullish message. If volume decreases during an uptrend, it could hint at the potential tapering off that trend.

Shifting focus to **open interest**, this metric presents the cumulative count of yet-to-be-settled contracts. It stands as a testament to an option's liquidity. A high count of open interest suggests pronounced trader commitment to that option, thereby simplifying initiating or concluding trades. Fluctuations in open interest offer a window into prevailing market sentiment. For instance, witnessing open interest grow with a price ascent is generally perceived as bullish. Swelling open interest paired with descending prices, conversely, tends to be interpreted as bearish.

Examining volume and open interest can give you invaluable perspectives on market mechanics, aiding in refining your trading strategies.

Sentiment Analysis

Market sentiment reflects investors' collective attitude or mood towards a specific market or financial instrument. It represents the balance between the number of investors who are optimistic about the market's future and those who are pessimistic. This sentiment can manifest as bullish, bearish, or neutral stances. Influences on market sentiment encompass a broad range of factors such as *economic data, earnings reports, geopolitical events,* and *other significant global occurrences.*

For options traders, awareness of market sentiment offers valuable insights. It not only provides a temperature check on the market's emotional state but also enables informed decision-making. A predominantly bullish sentiment often suggests optimism and could indicate a potential rise in market prices, making call options more appealing. In contrast, a bearish sentiment, driven by widespread pessimism, could lead to a price decline, favoring put options.

Sentiment Indicators and Contrarian Trading

Various tools and metrics aid in quantifying and understanding market sentiment. **Sentiment indicators** encompass tools ranging from volatility indices, such as the VIX, which gauges market volatility and is often termed the *"fear index,"* to the put/call ratio, which measures the trading volume of put options to call options. Surveys of investor sentiment can also provide a qualitative overview of prevailing market moods. Tracking and interpreting these indicators gives you insights to anticipate potential market movements.

Contrarian trading emerges from the premise that market crowd behavior can lead to price anomalies. Contrarian investors adopt positions opposing the prevailing market sentiment. They believe widespread sentiment, be it overly optimistic or pessimistic, can skew asset prices away from their intrinsic values. When most investors are pessimistic about a particular asset, driving its price down, contrarians see this as a potential buying opportunity, predicting that the asset is undervalued. As optimism reigns and asset prices soar, contrarian traders might see an overvaluation and consider selling or taking a short position. This philosophy can be applied in options trading by taking positions contrary to the prevailing sentiment leveraging options strategies to capitalize on anticipated price corrections.

The Role of Market Psychology in Options Trading

Market psychology significantly influences the dynamics of options trading. This concept encompasses the market's collective sentiment or emotional state at specific moments. Various factors, including *greed, fear, prevailing circumstances,* and *market participants' expectations,* shape the overarching sentiment in the trading environment.

Contrary to the ideal scenarios posited by financial theories, where every market participant can access and act upon all pertinent information, real-world market behaviors often diverge from this model. Emotional responses and inherent biases of investors and traders frequently drive their actions. These emotions can lead to discernible market movement patterns, which might be foreseeable or offer opportunities.

Recognizing and interpreting the prevailing sentiment can facilitate better-informed decision-making, enhancing investment outcomes.

Chapter 4
Basic Options Trading Strategies

Exploring deeper into options trading, learn more about long calls and puts, covered calls and protective puts, and bull and bear spreads. These basic strategies, each with unique risk-reward profiles, are the building blocks for more complicated trading tactics. Understanding when and how to apply these strategies can enhance your trading prowess and potential for success.

Long Call and Long Put

Going long involves buying an option based on the belief that the underlying asset's price will either increase *(for call options)* or decrease *(for put options)*. Traders with strong beliefs about future market movements or specific assets often use this strategy.

Long Call

One of the main reasons driving the use of the long call strategy is a ***speculative assumption about an impending price rise*** of the underlying asset. Such assumptions often stem from assessments of market patterns, economic metrics, organizational performance metrics, and significant worldwide occurrences. Upon purchasing a call option, traders position themselves advantageously to harness potential benefits from the predicted upward trajectory. When this speculation does not materialize, the trader's potential downside remains confined to the outlay made for the option, known as the premium.

Leverage also strengthens the long-call strategy. This attribute enables traders to oversee a substantial position while committing to a comparatively modest financial investment. When deploying a long call, you can oversee a considerable quantity of shares with a minimal expense relative to outright stock acquisition. As these anticipations about the asset's price surge materialize, the ensuing returns could overshadow the preliminary expense linked to the option premium. Acknowledge that while leverage can enhance returns, it holds equal potential to escalate losses in scenarios where market movements diverge from expectations.

Risk and Reward Dynamics

Engaging in a long call strategy in options trading presents a distinctive risk-reward scenario. When initiating a long call, a trader's maximum risk is encapsulated by the premium expended to secure the option. Regardless of the performance of the underlying asset, losses will not surpass this premium.

In terms of rewards, the profit ceiling from a long call is limitless. With an increase in the underlying asset's price, the call option's value correspondingly rises, generating potential profits. Profits start accruing once the underlying asset's price surpasses the sum of the call option's strike price and the paid premium.

Such a framework, where losses have a definite limit, but profits do not, often motivates traders to engage in a long call strategy, particularly if they harbor a bullish sentiment towards the underlying asset.

Strategic Variations and Adjustments

The long call strategy, while simple, offers traders variations and adjustments based on market shifts or altered perspectives.

- **Rolling Up.** When the underlying asset witnesses a price surge and a trader perceives further growth potential, the *"roll up"* approach may be considered. This strategy entails divesting the current in-the-money call and acquiring another call with a higher strike price. Such a sequence secures the profit from the initial position and upholds a bullish outlook.
- **Rolling Out.** Approaching the expiration date with a sustained bullish sentiment on the underlying asset but needing more time might prompt a trader to *"roll out"* their position. This move involves liquidating the present option and securing another with a deferred expiration date.
- **Creating a Spread.** A considerable rise in the underlying asset's price that translates to profit from the long call might drive a trader to offload a higher strike price call option. This decision culminates in a *"bull call spread,"* which, while curtailing maximum profit potential, also diminishes the cost of the trade, making it resistant to time decay.
- **Early Exit.** Market influences, be it shifts in perspectives on the underlying asset or external determinants such as economic news, might prompt a trader to disengage from the long call position ahead of time, either to conserve capital or curtail losses.
- **Hedging with a Long Put.** A volatile market may compel a trader to supplement the long call position with a long put option, culminating in a straddle. This combined strategy offers protection against drastic price drops of the underlying asset.

Long Put

Traders opt for a long put strategy when there is an *expected price decline in the underlying asset.* Investors who have researched or analyzed market conditions and foresee a potential downward movement in the asset's value can leverage this strategy. By purchasing a put option, you can capitalize on the declining price, and the deeper the asset's price dives below the option's strike price, the higher the potential profit. This approach allows you to gain from declining markets without short-selling the stock, which could entail unlimited risks.

The strategy further gives the trader control over a large amount of the underlying asset for a fraction of its actual price, giving them leverage. The maximum loss they stand to incur is limited to the premium paid for the put option, making it a defined risk strategy.

Another compelling reason traders employ the long put strategy is its *hedging capabilities.* Suppose an investor possesses a portfolio of stocks or other assets. In that case, they might be concerned about short-term declines in the market, especially if there are signs or predictions of impending economic downturns or industry-specific challenges.

Investors can safeguard their portfolios by purchasing put options on assets they already own or on broader market indices. If the market does decline, any losses incurred from the fall in the value of their stocks could be offset, at least in part, by the gains from their long put positions.

For example, consider an investor who holds shares in a tech company but anticipates a temporary industry slump due to regulatory changes. By initiating a long put strategy, the investor can shield their portfolio from potential losses during this period. Once the put option expires, or if the anticipated downturn does not materialize, they can let it expire or close the position.

The long put acts as an insurance policy for one's portfolio. Just as one pays a premium for car or home insurance to protect against unforeseen damages, the premium of a put option can be viewed as a small price to guard a portfolio against adverse market movements.

Risk and Reward Dynamics

The risk associated with a long put position finds its definition in the premium paid for the put option. The maximum loss a trader can experience when buying a put option equals the premium paid. This confined risk offers many traders comfort, particularly when juxtaposed with potential losses from strategies such as short selling.

Regarding rewards, the profit potential of a long put can be extensive. As the price of the underlying asset dips, the put option's value often ascends. The more significant the price descent and the further it resides below the option's strike price, the more the put's value increases. In a theoretical scenario where a stock's price drops to zero, a rare event, the profit potential reaches its pinnacle. Still factor in the premium when calculating profits. The trade's break-even point equates to the strike price less the premium paid.

Strategic Variations and Adjustments

A direct long-put position offers numerous avenues for strategic variations and adjustments to bolster or alter the position:

- **Combination Strategies.** A long put is amenable to amalgamation with diverse trading stances. For instance, it is an effective hedge against a prolonged stock position.

Traders possessing shares in a company and apprehending a transitory price plummet can acquire a put option. In the event of the stock depreciating, the surge in the put's value can counterbalance the stock's losses, either partially or wholly.
- **Early Exercise or Sale.** When the put option gains substantial value preceding its expiration, induced by a pronounced decline in the underlying asset's price, traders may opt for an early exercise or even sell the option to realize profits.
- **Married Put.** Involves buying an underlying stock and simultaneously buying put options for equivalent shares. This technique protects against short-term declines and can be beneficial if one is optimistic about the stock's long-term prospects.

Understanding the Major Option Greeks for Risk Management

While understanding the basic mechanics of option trading is essential, the Greeks provide insight into the various risks associated with option positions and how price movement, volatility, and time can affect an option's value. Knowing how to interpret and use these Greeks can differentiate between a successful trade and a loss, particularly for those holding long call or put positions.

Delta

Delta indicates how much the price of an option is expected to move in tandem with a $1 movement in its underlying asset. The delta is typically positive for call options, which means the option price will likely increase as the underlying asset price increases. In put options, the delta is usually negative, meaning the option price might decrease as the underlying asset price rises.

Applying delta in trading can aid in position sizing. Traders can assess the potential change in their option's value for a given movement in the underlying asset and adjust their position based on risk tolerance.

Gamma

Gamma measures how much the delta of an option is expected to change with every $1 movement in the underlying asset. It is particularly significant for at-the-money options, where the strike price is close to the current market price of the underlying asset. These options tend to have higher gamma values, making them more sensitive to price changes in the asset.

For traders, gamma helps gauge the risk associated with their delta exposure. A rapidly changing delta could lead to higher potential profits and losses. By monitoring gamma, traders can understand how their risk profile might change as the underlying asset moves.

Theta

Theta quantifies the effect of time's passage on an option's value. As options approach their expiration date, their value can decrease, a concept known as time decay. Theta provides a numerical value for this decay, reflecting how much an option's value might drop day by day. Typically, an option will have a negative theta, indicating its value will likely decrease over time.

For longer-term option positions, understanding theta is essential. Traders holding options with high negative theta values might see their positions lose value rapidly as expiration approaches, making it crucial to consider this when planning a trading strategy.

Vega

Vega measures how sensitive an option's value is to changes in the underlying asset's implied volatility (IV). A change in IV can significantly impact an option's price, even if the underlying asset's price remains unchanged. Both long calls and puts generally have a positive Vega, indicating they might gain value if IV increases.

For traders, monitoring Vega can provide insights into their position's vulnerability to shifts in market volatility. If they expect volatility to increase, holding options with high positive Vega values might be beneficial. However, a sudden drop in IV can adversely impact these positions, highlighting the importance of using Vega for risk assessment.

Covered Call and Protective Put

Covered calls and protective puts are basic options strategies that can help traders make money and protect themselves from risks when the market is right. To use these strategies well, you need to know how they work and when to use them.

The Covered Call Strategy

The covered call strategy involves owning the stock upon which it is based. After purchasing the stock, you sell call options for that stock. This action is considered *"covered"* because owning the stock fulfills the obligation of selling the call options. The primary objective is to earn from the option premiums rather than solely from an increase in the stock's price.

For each option sold, it corresponds to 100 shares of the stock. When setting a strike price for the options, it should be higher than the stock's current price, placing the calls in an *"out-of-the-money"* position. The revenue generated from selling these options can offset potential stock value decreases.

Should the stock price increase, the profit potential is capped at the chosen strike price. If the stock's closing price exceeds the strike price at option expiration, the call option buyer might exercise the option, claiming the shares. The option premium, however, remains with the seller regardless of the outcome.

This strategy suits stocks with moderate prices and a consistent trading history. Ideally, stocks should display a slight upward trend or maintain stability during the option holding period. Analyzing historical price movements can guide the selection of strike prices and option expiration dates, optimizing premium collection while minimizing associated risks.

Tweaking the strategy involves dealing with options that are deeper *"in-the-money"* or further *"out-of-the-money."* Consider time's impact on option values and the prevailing market uncertainty. Reduced market volatility might lead to diminished option premiums, warranting caution. Quick upward stock movements might necessitate strategic adjustments. Mastery over covered calls requires consistent practice.

Covered calls are advantageous in a moderately bullish market or during lateral market movements. They can provide a protective layer against losses for stocks with moderate upward potential. The strategy also offers profit opportunities if the stock appreciates and can enhance income in a stagnant market. Its limitation lies in capping significant profit potentials, necessitating judicious application, particularly with high-confidence stocks.

The Protective Put Strategy

The protective put strategy offers a technique to navigate volatile markets effectively. By integrating stock ownership with the purchase of put options, it aims to reduce downside risk. Puts provide an opportunity to sell shares at a predetermined strike price, ensuring investment protection while preserving the stock's potential for growth.

To adopt this position, ***secure the puts*** after obtaining the stock. Ensure the number of puts corresponds with the number of shares, with a single option corresponding to 100. ***Opt for a strike price*** mirroring the stock's prevailing price. Aligning the strike in this manner optimizes the put's value when the stock price decreases. ***Allocate complete cash reserves for the puts***, sidestepping the use of margin, which could lead to unforeseen liquidation.

These puts function akin to insurance, setting a ceiling on losses defined by the strike price. This mechanism provides a cushion, enabling stock retention even amidst market volatility. Should the stock ascend, the puts become inconsequential, resulting in gains limited only by the expended put premium.

Acquiring puts can be demanding for stocks with a hefty price tag. Evaluate the expense of the protection conferred before venturing into a trade. This strategy is best suited for stocks ardently committed over the long term. Steer clear of stocks prone to insolvency or those that necessitate stringent upkeep. Vigilant position management is necessary; adjust strikes during stock upswings and renews puts upon their expiration.

Employ methods such as technical analysis, particularly support and resistance levels, to pinpoint apt strike prices. Track implied volatility to discern optimal entry points. Pin down expiration dates that resonate with anticipated periods of market fluctuation. The overarching objective is to strike a balance, mitigating risk while harnessing the growth potential of well-understood stocks.

Effectively, when curating a portfolio, incorporating protective puts assists in addressing widespread market uncertainties. It facilitates the safeguarding of pivotal positions without the need for divestment. This allows for fruitful investment retention and potential amplification, all while instituting a comprehensive risk containment strategy.

Risk Management with Covered Calls and Protective Puts

Covered calls and protective puts inherently manage risk through their structures. With *covered calls*, your long stock offsets the short call obligation. Any stock drop is partly cushioned by premium income. The sale locks in partial profits upfront.

However, the stock can still fall below your purchase price, resulting in a loss. Upside is also capped by the strike price. Analyze the breakeven including premiums received. Appropriate position sizing, stop losses, and spread widths help control risk.

For *protective puts*, your maximum loss is the strike price minus stock cost plus put premium. Substantial opportunity costs can occur. Avoid overpaying for puts. Compare the put cost to just selling the stock and rebuying after a correction. Leverage your stock expertise to time trades well.

Weigh risk-reward carefully before trading. Contextualize the profit being capped versus premiums earned or hedging benefits obtained. Ensure adequate compensation for the defined risks. Containing risk means lost opportunity in exchange for greater certainty. Judge trades accordingly.

The vital relationship between risk and reward holds immense significance in options trading. Traders must take a probabilistic perspective. Consider the full range of risk-defined outcomes, and assess if the probabilities justify the trade. There are no perfect trades, but a fine process converts uncertainty into opportunity.

Bull and Bear Spreads

Bull and bear spreads are vertical spread strategies that limit risk while providing options traders defined profit potential. Mastering bull and bear spreads is key for traders seeking reduced risks while still benefiting from market trends in either direction.

Bull Spreads

Bull spreads entail the simultaneous execution of two positions: buying and selling options with identical expiration dates but varied strike prices.

There are two main methods to configure a bull spread:

1. **Using Call Options:** Purchasing a call option at a certain strike price and selling another at a superior strike price restricts potential profit to the difference between these strike prices, reduced by the net premium expended. The possible loss is confined to the net premium disbursed for the spread. This strategy seeks to profit from the premium difference as the underlying asset's price ascends.
2. **Using Put Options:** This method involves selling a put option at an elevated strike price and buying another at a reduced strike price. The potential profit and loss both have ceilings. This strategy aims to benefit from the premium difference as the underlying asset's price increases.

Bull spreads prove advantageous in markets that do not anticipate substantial price fluctuations. Their inherent limit on profit and loss offers traders a safety net, making it a preferred strategy for those targeting a particular price level for the underlying asset.

Bear Spreads

Bear spreads engage traders expecting a bearish move in the underlying asset. This strategy also necessitates the concurrent execution of two option positions, but the intent differs, focusing on profiting from a reduction in the underlying asset's price.

There are two main methods to configure a bear spread:

1. **Using Call Options:** Selling a call option at an inferior strike price while buying another at a superior strike price limits the potential profit to the net premium received, adjusted by the difference between the two strike prices. The maximal loss is bound by the difference in strike prices less the net premium received. This strategy pursues gains from the premium difference as the underlying asset's price drops.
2. **Using Put Options:** This involves purchasing a put option at a superior strike price and selling another at an inferior strike price. As the underlying asset's price descends, the difference in the premiums of the two options can yield profit. Both potential profit and loss have boundaries.

Risk and Reward of Bull and Bear Spreads

Both spreads offer traders a structured approach to options trading, encapsulating risk and profit potentials. With *bull spreads*, the peak of profit realization aligns with the underlying asset's price meeting or surpassing the higher strike price upon expiration. The greatest loss is realized when the underlying asset's price meets or descends below the lower strike price upon expiration.

Turning to *bear spreads*, traders find the pinnacle of profitability when the underlying asset's price meets or drops below the lower strike price at expiration. The gravest loss is encountered when the underlying asset's price reaches or surpasses the higher strike price upon expiration.

In both strategies, the maximum profit and loss are known in advance. This makes bull and bear spreads popular among traders who want to limit their risk while still having the potential for a reasonable profit.

Chapter 5
Advanced Options Trading Strategies

In this chapter, explore more complex options and strategies for skilled traders. Each strategy requires understanding when to utilize them, how they are constructed, and their inherent risk-reward dynamics. With mastery of these advanced strategies, you can better adapt to shifting market conditions and capitalize on various opportunities. The intricacies of straddles, condors, butterflies, and complex spreads are uncovered in this chapter.

Straddles and Strangles

In options trading, certain strategies stand out for their potential to profit from high volatility. Two such strategies are the straddles and strangles.

The Long Straddle Strategy

In an unpredictable market where significant volatility is expected, the long straddle strategy provides an approach that can harness potential price movements. This strategy encompasses the concurrent purchase of a call option and a put option on the same underlying asset, having identical strike prices and expiration dates. Such a configuration provides an opportunity to profit from considerable price fluctuations, regardless of the direction.

Consider an underlying stock that is currently priced at $50. An impending earnings report suggests a substantial price move, but the direction of this move—*positive or negative*—is uncertain. To leverage this anticipated volatility, one might acquire a call and a put option, each with a strike price of $50 and a one-month expiration.

This leads to two possible outcomes:

- **The stock price rises significantly.** When the stock appreciates significantly, moving to, for example, $60, the call option's value rises, facilitating a profit from this uptrend. While the put option might lose its entire value, the potential appreciation of the call option should cover and exceed this loss.
- **The stock price drops significantly.** As the stock declines sharply, descending to $40, the put option becomes more valuable, presenting a potential profit avenue from this downtrend. Although the call option might be worthless, the put option's potential gains are likely substantial enough to cover this.

Break-Even Points and Profit Potential

Analyzing the break-even points for the long straddle is essential to gauge its profitability. The underlying asset's price must shift more than the aggregate amount spent on the premiums. The strategy has two break-even points:

- **Upper Break-Even Point.** Calculated by adding the total premiums paid to the call's strike price.
- **Lower Break-Even Point.** Deduced by subtracting the total premiums paid from the put's strike price.

A feature of the long straddle is the limitless profit potential it offers. As the price deviates further from the strike price, the profit potential rises correspondingly.

Practical Tips for Implementing the Long Straddle

The long straddle holds favor among traders who anticipate sizeable price movements but remain uncertain about the direction. Even though many are acquainted with the fundamental mechanics of the long straddle, its optimized execution mandates thorough attention to detail and a careful weighing of multiple aspects.

- **Importance of Timing.** The success of the long straddle often rests heavily on precise timing. Identifying signs or impending events that might induce significant price fluctuations in the underlying asset is needed. Prime examples include *earnings announcements, regulatory outcomes,* or *major economic data releases*. Establishing the straddle before such occurrences can amplify the probability of tapping into pronounced price dynamics.
- **Keeping an Eye on Volatility.** Option premiums could be relatively economical when the implied volatility exceeds historical measures. This scenario might present a more opportune moment to initiate a long straddle.
- **Deliberations on Expiration Dates.** The chosen expiration date for the options in a long straddle can influence both the incurred cost and the prospective profit. Longer expiration dates generally command higher prices but offer an extended window for the expected price movement. Swiftly approaching expiration dates might come cheaper, but they proffer a limited duration for a price shift.
- **Risk Management Endeavors.** Setting predefined profit thresholds or maximum loss limits at which to conclude the positions provides clarity. Given that a long straddle

entails purchasing two long options, the potential loss, equivalent to the premiums paid, is definite. Overseeing the strategy and adhering to an exit blueprint can avert unwarranted losses.

- **Commitment to Staying Updated.** Consistently refreshing one's knowledge of news and events with potential ramifications on the underlying asset is essential. Possessing an information advantage can yield valuable insights into prospective price oscillations, facilitating adept strategy modifications or exits.
- **Insights from the Greeks.** For practitioners of the long straddle, the Theta, representing time decay, can bear substantial relevance. As options edge closer to their expiration, they undergo value depreciation. This phenomenon can impact the strategy's profitability, particularly if the forecasted price movement remains unrealized.
- **Scrutinizing Liquidity Levels.** Options characterized by high liquidity frequently exhibit tighter bid-ask spreads, reducing the costs linked to trade initiation and conclusion.
- **Curtailing Excessive Exposure.** Allocating an overly generous portion of one's trading capital to a singular long straddle is inadvisable. Spreading investments across diverse strategies and underlying assets aids a more balanced risk management approach.

The Long Strangle Strategy

The long strangle strategy involves purchasing an out-of-the-money call option and an out-of-the-money put option on the same underlying asset with identical expiration dates. The call option possesses a strike price above the asset's current market price, while the put option has its strike price below the current market price. This combination creates an avenue to profit from pronounced price movements in any direction.

For illustration, consider a stock with a current market value of $100. An anticipated event, a vital product launch, or an impending regulatory verdict might trigger a marked price movement. The direction of this movement, however, remains uncertain. To exploit the expected volatility, you could buy a call option with a strike price of $110 and a put option with a strike price of $90, both set to expire in a month. There are two potential scenarios:

When the stock's price escalates to $120, the value of the call option increases, leading to a profit from the upward price shift. Although the put option may become worthless, the profit from the call option can offset this loss.

In contrast, if the stock price diminishes to $80, the value of the put option rises, resulting in a profit from the downward movement. The call option might become valueless, but the earnings from the put option can compensate for this.

The long strangle strategy presents several advantages:

- **Flexibility.** This strategy allows a broader scope for potential gains than the long straddle because the asset can undergo extensive movement in either direction before reaching the break-even points.
- **Affordable Premiums.** As the strategy involves purchasing out-of-the-money options, the premiums tend to be less than the premiums for at-the-money options, which are used in the long straddle.
- **Vast Profit Potential.** There is limitless profit potential on the upward side and considerable potential on the downside, limited only by the asset's value decreasing to zero.

Practical Tips for the Long Strangle

Below are some tips to maximize long strangle's potential in volatile markets.

- **Recognizing Favorable Market Conditions.** The long strangle benefits most from volatile market scenarios. Uncertain events, such as *earnings releases, geopolitical occurrences,* or *central bank announcements,* often result in dramatic price shifts that this strategy capitalizes on. Here, the direction of the move is less important than its magnitude.
- **Strike Price Selection.** A call option, forecasting an upward price movement, should have its strike above the current asset price. In contrast, anticipating a downward movement, the put option should be set below the market price. The differential between these strikes and the ongoing market price determines potential gains and risks.
- **Timing the Expiration.** With this strategy entailing the purchase of two out-of-the-money options, time decay's impact is heightened. A common approach to countering this is opting for options with extended expiration, allowing sufficient room for desired market movements.
- **Efficient Cost Management.** With the dual purchase of options, two premiums become payable. Efficiently managing these costs enhances profitability. Ways to achieve this include *monitoring the bid-ask spreads, using brokerage benefits,* and *focusing on highly liquid underlying assets.*
- **Embracing Continuous Learning.** Given the fluid nature of financial markets, updating oneself becomes a necessity. Evaluate the strategy, draw lessons from past trades, and track market shifts. This ongoing learning can enhance the strategy's success rate over time.

Iron Condors and Butterflies

The iron condor and butterfly are neutral options strategies ideal for range-bound markets. Mastering these strategies allows capitalizing on volatile sideways markets while defining risk parameters. Both can become tools for traders seeking non-directional options plays with practice.

The Iron Condor Strategy

The name of the Iron Condor strategy draws inspiration from the condor bird, renowned for its expansive wingspan and ability to glide with minimal effort. This trait of effortless gliding mirrors the strategy's objective to capitalize on a stable market without drastic price movements.

The Iron Condor integrates two vertical spreads: one catering to a *mildly bullish sentiment* and the other to a *mildly bearish sentiment*. A feature of this setup is the incorporation of out-of-the-money options, which focus solely on their time value, without intrinsic value.

Initiating the Iron Condor provides traders with a net credit. This arises from the difference in the options sold and bought premiums. This acquired net credit epitomizes the apex of potential profit for traders, should the strategy pan out as desired.

The most favorable outcome materializes when the underlying asset's price remains sandwiched between the two central strike prices as the expiration approaches. In such circumstances, all options expire without value, permitting traders to retain the net credit received initially. The relationship between the asset price and the chosen strike prices plays a pivotal role in determining the success of this strategy.

While the Iron Condor strategy aims to exploit market stability, it is not immune to risks. The gravest risk emerges if the underlying asset's price veers past the farthest strike prices. Here, the potential loss equates to the difference in strike prices of one of the spreads, adjusted by the acquired net credit.

This strategy finds its niche in predictably calm market environments where significant price oscillations are not in the forecast. Markets that exhibit a consistent price trajectory offer the ideal backdrop for the Iron Condor. Volatility, especially on the lower end, enhances the strategy's prospects.

Markets can be unpredictable, and there may arise situations where traders find the need to recalibrate the Iron Condor. Some common adjustments encompass rolling out a side that faces challenges or shifting strike prices. For those seeking added maneuverability, variants of the Iron Condor exist, such as the unbalanced version, which does not maintain symmetry between put and call spreads.

A trader may not linger until expiration to conclude their position. Should the asset's price gravitate dangerously close to one of the extreme strike prices, prudence might dictate an early exit or an adjustment to curb potential losses. The impending expiration can also induce changes in the strategy's behavior, prompting decisive actions.

While the Iron Condor is unique, it exhibits similarities with other strategies. For example, the butterfly spread, like the Iron Condor, aims to benefit from limited price movements. But the Iron Condor's inherent structure, combining two vertical spreads, introduces distinction, especially in premium asset and risk control.

Reflecting on historical market trends, there have been instances where the Iron Condor strategy demonstrated its mettle. Visualize a tech stock, stable and trading within a narrow band for consecutive months. Many traders set up Iron Condors, anchored in their conviction of the stock's sustained stability. As the expiration dawned and the stock price persisted within anticipated boundaries, these traders reaped their maximum profit, underscoring the strategy's potential when wielded aptly.

The Butterfly Spread Strategy

Tracing back, the Butterfly Spread has roots in the foundational concepts of options trading. Its emergence answered traders' need to capitalize on specific market conditions—particularly those characterized by limited price movement. The very essence of this strategy hinges on creating a position that can benefit from a stable market, mirroring the equilibrium and balance often sought by traders in volatile environments.

There are ***call and put butterfly spreads***. While both play on the same theme of limited price movement, their structures diverge based on whether they incorporate calls or puts. The ***Iron Butterfly***, another variant, matches the concept by using both calls and puts simultaneously, offering a distinctive risk and reward setup compared to its traditional counterparts.

Initiating a Butterfly Spread demands precision. Begin with selecting the right strike prices. As three are involved, their proximity to the current price and each other plays a role in determining the potential outcome. The spacing between these strikes can further influence the strategy's potential profit and loss, making it an essential factor to ponder.

Not all market conditions, however, are ripe for the Butterfly Spread. Its ideal backdrop is a market where drastic price swings are not on the horizon—essentially a stable or range-bound market. Factors such as time decay, which erodes the value of options as expiration approaches, play into the hands of the Butterfly Spread, especially if prices remain stable. Likewise, low volatility environments amplify the chances of success for this strategy.

Markets are dynamic, and shifts can occur even with the best predictions. If a Butterfly Spread starts to deviate from its expected path, traders might need interventions. Adjustments, such as rolling out positions to future months or re-establishing the spreads at different strike prices, can come to the rescue. Manage and limit potential losses or realign the strategy with revised market expectations.

There are times when it is advantageous to exit a Butterfly Spread before expiration. This decision might be triggered by the underlying asset's price nearing one of the outer strikes or other market signals indicating potential threats to the position. When contemplating an early exit, traders must weigh the costs of closing the position against potential benefits or risk mitigation.

For traders who have specific market views, advanced Butterfly Spread versions exist. The **Broken-Wing Butterfly**, for instance, skews risk and reward by having uneven distances between strike prices. Meanwhile, the **Unbalanced Butterfly Spread** varies the number of contracts used, introducing an asymmetry in potential profits and losses. These advanced strategies cater to nuanced market views and individual risk preferences.

Common Pitfalls and Recommendations

Even seasoned traders sometimes stumble when implementing the Iron Condors and Butterflies Spread strategy. Recognizing common pitfalls can lead to more informed trading decisions.

- **Avoiding Overconfidence.** Just because a particular setup has worked in the past does not guarantee future success. Always analyze each trade on its merit, and stay focused.

- **Overtrading.** Increasing the frequency of trades or the amount of capital allocated can be tempting, especially after a streak of successful trades. However, overtrading can expose a trader to unnecessary risks. Sticking to a disciplined approach is essential, irrespective of recent successes or failures.
- **Ignoring Fees.** The Iron Condor and Butterflies strategies involve multiple legs, which means various transactions. Overlooking the cumulative effect of brokerage fees on these trades can eat into profits. Using a broker that offers competitive rates is wise, especially when frequently employing multi-leg strategies.
- **Neglecting Early Exit.** If the market starts moving aggressively against a position, closing out or adjusting the trade to manage risks might be wise.
- **Recommendation for Success.** One of the most recommended practices is continuous education. The options market is vast, and strategies evolve. Regularly refreshing knowledge, back-testing strategies, and learning from successes and failures can pave the way for sustained success in employing the Iron Condors and Butterflies Spread strategy.

Calendar and Diagonal Spreads

Calendar and diagonal spreads take advantage of differing time decays between contract expirations. The intricacies of these spreads are uncovered in this section.

The Calendar Spread Strategy

The Calendar Spread emerges as a tactical response to time decay differentials between options. Its rise in popularity was observed in contexts where traders envisioned limited short-term asset movement juxtaposed against ambiguous longer-term prospects.

Traders are often drawn to the Calendar Spread for its semblance of psychological reprieve. By producing positions that optimize time decay, there is an inherent sense of aligning oneself with the natural rhythm of time. The strategy pivots on the variances in decay rates between options of different maturities, laying down a path to harness these discrepancies for profit.

Adapting to multifaceted market moods, the Calendar Spread exhibits commendable flexibility. Bullish phases see a leaning towards call calendar spreads, while bearish phases bring put calendar spreads to the fore. In a market that lacks a clear directional bias, the strategy can lean on both calls and puts to extract value from time decay. As market sentiments ebb and flow, adept traders often recalibrate by adjusting strike prices or rolling options.

Central to understanding the Calendar Spread is grasping its risk and reward interplay. The prospect of peak gains materializes when the underlying asset aligns with the options' strike price as the short-term option reaches expiration. Yet, a marked movement in the underlying asset, irrespective of direction, risks undermining the strategy's efficacy irrespective of direction.

The initiation of a Calendar Spread usually coincides with the trader's assessment of muted short-term volatility juxtaposed against a nebulous longer-term trajectory. Triggers for strategy dissolution or adaptation might include pronounced asset price shifts or situations where the longer-term option's decay does not sufficiently counterbalance the imminent expiration of the short-term option.

Volatility significantly sways the strategy's fortunes, especially of the implied variety. A swell in implied volatility generally augments the strategy, given the pronounced Vega of longer-dated options in contrast to their shorter-dated counterparts. The intricacies of volatility skews also merit attention, influencing relative option pricing across varying expiries.

Vigilance forms the cornerstone of effective strategy management. Market turbulence or significant asset shifts necessitate prompt recalibration. Typical corrective measures encompass rolling the soon-to-expire option to a distant date or rejigging strike prices.

Historical deployments of the Calendar Spread provide intriguing insights. A case in point is its application in stable pharmaceutical stocks, especially those on the cusp of pivotal FDA decisions slated for the distant future. Here, traders leveraged the Calendar Spread to ride out short-term tranquility, retaining the optionality for potential longer-term gyrations.

The Diagonal Spread Strategy

The Diagonal Spread found its footing in options trading by integrating principles from renowned strategies. Drawing from the methodical essence of vertical spreads and the temporal aspect of calendar spreads, it crafted a distinct strategy tailor-made for particular market situations.

For those gravitating towards the Diagonal Spread, the essence lies in choosing apt options. The procedure emphasizes a harmonious blend of unique expiration dates and diverse strike prices. This blend serves as the heart of the strategy, articulating its core benefits.

The Diagonal Spread can use dual profit channels: *options' intrinsic time decay* and *pronounced price variations of the underlying asset*. The architecture of the strategy facilitates a premium income from the short-term option sale, serving dual purposes: *mitigating the upfront financial outlay* and *enhancing the strategy's economic viability*.

Venturing beyond immediate intricacies, the long-term option in the Diagonal Spread exudes potential. Its valuation is closely knitted with the prolonged directional tendencies of the asset. The disparity between the chosen strike prices and the real-time price progression of the asset sculpts the profit spectrum here.

The Diagonal Spread's adaptability shines, accommodating varied market moods, whether bullish, bearish, or stagnant. Fine-tuning the strategy becomes imperative with shifting market insights and asset price forecasts to resonate with the trader's vision.

Despite the strategy's inherent strengths, market unpredictability remain a challenge. The accrued premium from the short-lived option functions as a defensive mechanism, curbing specific risks. Remain alert to scenarios where unanticipated market forces might breach these defenses, invoking possible setbacks.

The calculus of deciding position terminations or modifications is a delicate interplay of market rhythms and strategic insights. Key determinants like forthcoming market transitions or option expirations shape these decisions. A discerning trader judiciously navigates these factors, preserving the strategy's harmony with the market's pulse.

Chapter 6
Risk Management in Options Trading

Risk management is vital when trading options, given their inherent complexity and leverage. This chapter overviews options trading risks, risk assessment methodologies, and risk mitigation techniques. Explore the different types of risk, how to gauge risk through volatility and probability analysis, effective position sizing, utilizing stop losses, and hedging. The role of diversification in balancing risks is examined in depth, including diversification benefits and strategies, as well as limitations.

Understanding and Assessing Risk

Options trading carries substantial risks that require careful evaluation.

Types of Risks

In options trading, various risks await, each demanding its strategic response, such as:

- **Price Risk.** Price movements in the underlying asset bring about this risk. When the asset moves contrary to your prediction, there is potential for a loss as your option might expire without value. Keeping abreast of market dynamics and events that could sway the asset's price can mitigate this.

- **Time Decay Risk (Theta).** As the clock ticks, options shed value, even if other variables stay unchanged. This decline in value, termed as theta, intensifies as expiration looms. One could counter this by leaning towards trades of shorter duration or by adjusting positions as the expiration date draws close.
- **Volatility Risk (Vega).** Volatility gauges the pace and extent of price shifts in the underlying asset. An abrupt surge or drop in volatility can markedly alter an option's price. Navigate this risk by observing implied volatility, which provides insights into anticipated future volatility based on prevailing option prices. Strategies such as straddles or strangles might be apt in the face of predicted volatility jumps.
- **Interest Rate Risk (Rho).** Changes in interest rates, though a subtler risk, can sway option prices. A general trend is observed wherein call options may appreciate with rising interest rates, whereas put options might see depreciation. Being in the loop about central bank stances and pertinent economic indicators can offer foresight into prospective interest rate shifts.
- **Liquidity Risk.** Certain options might not witness frequent trading, posing challenges when attempting to transact without influencing the price. Before initiating a trade, ascertain the option's liquidity by scrutinizing its bid-ask spread and volume of trades. Options characterized by tighter bid-ask spreads and a robust trading volume are typically more liquid.
- **Early Assignment Risk.** This risk is particularly for American-style options, where there is a possibility of the option being exercised ahead of its expiration. Such early exercises are often observed with deep-in-the-money options or leading to a dividend declaration. Preemptive measures include rolling the position or earmarking funds to address the assignment.

- **Counterparty Risk.** The opposing party in the options contract may default on their commitments. While exchanges and clearinghouses largely negate this risk in standardized options, it remains a consideration, especially in the over-the-counter markets.
- **Leg Risk.** For strategies involving multiple options, there is a chance that while one leg of the trade is executed, another might not be. Such scenarios can inadvertently result in an undesired open position. Employing combination orders, such as vertical spreads or iron condors, ensures simultaneous execution of all trade components.

Assessing Risk

Below are some factors to consider when assessing risk in options trading:

- **Define Your Risk Tolerance.** Before diving into any trade, understand your risk appetite. *Are you comfortable with high-risk, high-reward scenarios or prefer more conservative trades?* By determining your risk tolerance, you can select strategies that align with your comfort level.
- **Analyze the Underlying Asset.** The risk of an option is intrinsically linked to its underlying asset. Research the asset's historical price movements, earnings reports, and any upcoming events that might influence its price. Doing so will give you a clearer picture of the potential price volatility.
- **Use Technical Analysis.** Charts, trend lines, and technical indicators can provide insights into potential price movements. For instance, if an underlying asset approaches a resistance level, it might face selling pressure. Recognizing these patterns can help you anticipate potential risks.
- **Consider Implied Volatility.** Implied volatility reflects the market's expectation of future price volatility. A

higher implied volatility suggests that traders expect significant price swings, which can impact the option's price. Comparing an option's implied volatility to its historical volatility gauges the market's sentiment.

- **Calculate the Maximum Loss.** Before entering any trade, determine the maximum amount you could lose. For most options strategies, the maximum loss is the premium paid. However, the potential loss can be substantial for strategies like selling naked options. Always ensure that you are comfortable with the worst-case scenario.
- **Factor in Time Decay.** Remember that options are time-sensitive. The closer an option gets to its expiration date, the faster its time value erodes. Assess how time decay might impact your trade, especially if you hold an option close to expiration.
- **Evaluate Liquidity.** An option's liquidity can impact your ability to enter or exit trades. Assess the bid-ask spread and trading volume. A narrower spread and higher volume typically indicate better liquidity, reducing the risk of slippage.
- **Consider External Factors.** Economic events, interest rate decisions, and geopolitical tensions can all influence the options market. Stay informed about upcoming events that might impact your trades. This proactive approach can help you anticipate and mitigate potential risks.
- **Use Risk Assessment Tools.** Many trading platforms offer tools that can help you assess the risk of a particular trade. These tools can provide insights into potential profit and loss scenarios, allowing you to make more informed decisions.
- **Always Have an Exit Strategy.** Before entering any trade, know when and how you will exit. Be it taking profits at a certain level or cutting losses, having a clear exit strategy can help you manage risks effectively.

Risk Management Techniques

Two key techniques can be utilized in managing risks, such as:

Position Sizing and Stop Loss Orders

Position sizing can be compared to determining the fuel required based on the distance and your vehicle's efficiency. Overestimating can lead to wasted resources, while underestimating might halt your journey. In options trading, allocating excessive capital to a single trade exposes you to high losses, while an overly cautious approach might mean missed profit opportunities.

Seasoned traders often follow the 1% to 2% rule. This guideline dictates that only 1% to 2% of the total trading capital should be at risk for any trade. For example, with a trading account of $50,000, the risk per trade should be confined to $500 to $1,000. This approach ensures that a string of less favorable trades will not severely impact your capital.

While position sizing highlights the investment amount, stop-loss orders determine the point to exit a trade to mitigate further losses. A stop-loss order can be visualized as a safety net, a preset price level triggering the sale of an asset to limit potential losses. By establishing this limit, you commit to an exit strategy if a trade moves unfavorably, ensuring decisions remain unclouded by emotions.

Implementing a stop-loss involves an understanding of the asset's volatility, past behavior, and prevailing market conditions. For instance, a volatile option might necessitate a broader stop-loss to accommodate its price fluctuations. In contrast, a stable option might be managed with a narrower stop-loss.

A key benefit of integrating position sizing with stop-loss orders lies in its clear strategy for trades. Before initiating a position, the risk and exit points are already established, fostering confidence and promoting disciplined trading.

In essence, position sizing and stop-loss orders complement each other. The former focuses on capital allocation, while the latter outlines the limits of that allocation. Together, they create a comprehensive risk management framework, offering stability in the face of market uncertainties.

Using Options for Hedging

Options provide inherent leverage, making them suitable instruments for hedging. Hedging with options entails adopting a counteractive position to one's current stance, aiming to neutralize potential losses. Delving into this concept offers clarity.

Consider an individual owning a significant number of shares in Company A. Over the past year, the shares have appreciated due to a consistent rise in the company's stock price. Recent market dynamics or an impending earnings report might indicate a potential short-term dip in the stock's value. Rather than liquidating the shares, which could result in tax implications and the loss of potential future gains, options can serve as a protective measure.

A direct method for this protection is acquiring a put option on the stock. Owning a put option grants the holder the right to sell the stock at a predetermined price within a designated timeframe without being bound to do so. When the stock's price experiences a downturn, the corresponding increase in the put option's value can counterbalance the stock's depreciation. As the stock's value remains unchanged or appreciates, the only financial drawback is the premium expended on the put.

Hedging extends beyond just stock protection. Options are versatile and can safeguard various investments, from commodities and bonds to other options. For example, an investor with a long call option, anticipating an asset's price elevation but wary of a short-term depreciation, might procure a put option as insurance. This tactic, termed a protective put, ensures that the asset's depreciation allows the put option to be utilized, thus counteracting losses.

In another situation, an individual with bond holdings might be apprehensive about escalating interest rates, leading to a decline in bond prices. As a protective measure against this, the investor might secure put options linked to an interest-rate futures contract. An escalation in interest rates resulting in a drop in bond prices correlates with an appreciation of the put options, neutralizing the bond's devaluation.

Investors need to comprehend both the advantages and implications of hedging. While hedging offers a buffer against unexpected market downturns, it does not assure profitability. The cumulative costs of option premiums, especially when protecting non-vulnerable positions, can be influential. A favorable market move might also see the hedging strategy curbing potential profits.

Diversification

Diversification is a key risk management technique in investing and trading. Rather than putting all capital on one or two trades, diversification spreads the risk over multiple positions and asset classes. In options trading, this can involve trading different underlying securities, utilizing various strategies *(spreads, straddles, condors)*, and balancing short and long positions. While diversification reduces risk, it also limits potential gains from any one position. In severe market declines, correlations across asset classes rise, and diversification benefits decline. Despite limits, diversification remains a cautious practice for long-term trading success.

The Benefits of Diversification

Offering various benefits, diversification enhances your trading experience.

- **Reduction of Systemic Risk.** Systemic risk is the possibility of a major collapse of the entire financial system or market, which can be hard to predict. By diversifying your options trades across different sectors or asset classes, you reduce the impact of a catastrophic event in any single sector on your portfolio. For instance, if you have options in the technology sector and there is a sudden tech market crash, having positions in healthcare or utilities can offset potential losses.
- **Access to Multiple Opportunities.** Different sectors and assets often have varied market cycles. While one might be in a downturn, another could be experiencing growth. Diversifying allows you to tap into multiple opportunities, ensuring you always have a stake in a prospering market segment.
- **Flexibility in Strategy Application.** Options trading is rich with strategies, from bullish and bearish to neutral. By diversifying, you are not just spreading across assets but also strategies. This means you can capitalize on various market conditions, be it a rising, falling, or stagnant market.
- **Mitigation of Unsystematic Risk.** Unlike systemic risk, which affects the entire market, unsystematic risk is specific to a particular company or industry. By diversifying your options portfolio, you dilute the impact of adverse events related to a particular company or sector. For instance, if a pharmaceutical company you have invested in fails to get FDA approval for a drug, having options in other sectors or companies can cushion this blow.

- **Enhanced Portfolio Returns.** While diversification is primarily about risk reduction, it can also enhance returns. Allocating investments across assets that are not perfectly correlated increases the chance of capitalizing on positive price movements in various sectors or assets.
- **Learning and Growth.** Diversifying also has an educational benefit. Exposing yourself to various assets and strategies gives you a broader understanding of market dynamics. This knowledge can be invaluable, honing your trading skills and intuition.

Start small by diversifying across sectors before delving into different strategies. Over time, as you become more comfortable and knowledgeable, you can further refine your approach.

Diversification Strategies

Some diversification strategies to implement include the following:

Asset Class Diversification

Different asset classes often respond differently to economic events. For instance, during periods of inflation, commodities like gold might perform well for you, while bonds might underperform. During economic downturns, stocks might decline, but government bonds or certain currencies might remain stable or even appreciate. By holding a mix of asset classes, you can cushion your portfolio against adverse movements in any single class. While you might be comfortable and familiar with stocks, venturing into commodities, currencies, and bonds can offer new opportunities. Commodities, for instance, can be influenced by supply-demand dynamics, geopolitical events, and weather patterns.

Currencies can provide insights into global economic health, interest rate differentials, and geopolitical tensions. Central bank policies, inflation expectations, and fiscal policies can influence bonds, especially government bonds. Different asset classes have different volatility profiles. Stocks are more volatile for you, while government bonds offer stability. Currencies can be influenced by macroeconomic data releases, making them volatile around specific events for you. By diversifying across asset classes, you can achieve a balance, ensuring your entire portfolio is not subject to the same volatility levels..

Sectoral Diversification

Different sectors can react differently to economic events, even within a specific asset class like stocks. For instance, during a technology boom, tech stocks might soar for you, but pharmaceuticals might take the lead during a healthcare crisis. Each sector has its own set of drivers. While technology might be driven by innovation, product launches, and regulatory challenges, oil prices, geopolitical tensions, and environmental policies might influence the energy sector.

Strategy Diversification

As different asset classes and sectors react differently to economic scenarios, trading strategies can perform differently under various market conditions. A bullish strategy might work well in a rising market but can lead to losses in a bearish or sideways market for you. By employing a mix of strategies, you can capitalize on various market conditions. For instance, while covered calls might be ideal for a moderately bullish market, straddles can be beneficial during periods of high volatility, and iron condors might be suitable for range-bound markets for you. Every strategy comes with its own set of risks. By diversifying across strategies, you can ensure that you are not overly exposed to the risks associated with any single strategy.

Time Horizon Diversification

Diversifying based on options' expiration dates is a strategic move that can help you balance risk and reward. By their nature, options come with an expiration date, and the time left until that date can impact their value for you. With their impending expiration, short-term options can be more sensitive to immediate market movements, making them both riskier and potentially more profitable for you. Long-term options, with their extended expiration dates, tend to be less reactive to short-term market fluctuations, offering you a more stable, albeit potentially less lucrative, investment. Holding a blend of short-term and long-term options, you can aim for quick gains while having a safety net in place for longer-term market developments.

Geographic Diversification

In the age of globalization, limiting your trading activities to a single country or region can be a missed opportunity for you. Different regions and countries have unique economic drivers, challenges, and growth prospects. By expanding your trading horizon beyond the United States and incorporating assets from Europe, Asia, or other emerging markets, you can tap into broader economic dynamics. This not only offers you more avenues for potential profit but also acts as a hedge against region-specific downturns or economic challenges. For instance, while the U.S. market might be facing headwinds, Asian markets might be on an upswing, and having exposure to both can balance out your portfolio's performance.

Volatility Diversification

Volatility, or the degree of variation in an asset's price, is a double-edged sword in trading for you. High volatility can mean higher profit potential for you, but it also comes with increased risk. Low-volatility assets offer you more stability but with limited profit potential. By diversifying based on volatility, you can aim for the best of both worlds. Options on high-volatility stocks can provide you the thrill of significant price swings, while those on low-volatility stocks can offer a steadier, more predictable return. This approach ensures that your entire portfolio is not at the mercy of wild market swings, providing a balanced risk-reward profile.

Size and Scale Diversification

The size of a company, often categorized as large-cap, mid-cap, or small-cap, can influence its stock's behavior and, by extension, the behavior of options on that stock for you. Large-cap companies, often industry leaders with established market positions, might offer stability but slower growth for you. Small-cap companies might be in their growth phase, offering the potential for higher returns but with increased risk for you. Mid-cap companies can fall somewhere in between for you. By diversifying based on company size, you can tap into different market segments with unique growth prospects and challenges. This diversification can provide a well-rounded portfolio for you, poised to capitalize on various market dynamics.

The Limits of Diversification

Diversification can *falter during extreme market events*. For instance, correlations between seemingly disparate assets might surge during financial crises. A diversified portfolio may still witness a decline in the value of its investments during such times.

Over-diversification presents another challenge. A portfolio with an abundance of options becomes challenging to manage and monitor. With an extensive array of options, say 100 different ones, overseeing each and making timely decisions about acquisitions and sales becomes complex, leading to missed prospects and less-than-ideal returns.

The benefits of diversification wane if there is a lack of understanding about the chosen assets or strategies. For instance, an inadequate grasp of options can result in costly blunders. Thorough research and comprehension of risks are essential before venturing into any asset or investment strategy.

Chapter 7
Trading Psychology and Discipline

Trading effectively requires mastery of both analytical skills and psychological control. Emotions like fear, greed, and bias can undermine success if not properly managed. Implementing risk management rules and other components into a comprehensive trading plan helps traders act methodically based on strategy, not emotion.

Plans must adapt to changing markets through ongoing review and adjustment. Maintaining strict discipline in following a trading plan also supports results, aided by lifestyle balance and other techniques. With psychological abilities to complement technical skills, traders are equipped to achieve consistent profitability in the face of inevitable trading challenges.

Emotional Challenges in Trading

Trading is an emotional rollercoaster. Euphoria from wins gives way to fear of losses. Greed tempts traders to overextend, while impatience breeds impulsive decisions. Cognitive biases distort market perceptions. Together, these forces conspire to undermine trading success. Yet with proper self-awareness, traders can control their emotions. Risk limits curb fear and greed. Checklists counter bias. Patience arises from trusting the trading plan. By mastering the inner game of trading, technical skills flourish.

Fear and Greed in Trading

Fear, originating from previous losses or impending market uncertainties, may inhibit trading actions. It could discourage entering a potentially profitable trade or lead to early exits from trades that could have yielded gains. Such fear reduces potential gains.

Conversely, greed presents its challenges. Seeing a profitable trade may encourage aspirations for even larger returns. This aspiration might keep traders engaged in a position for too long. With their unpredictability, financial markets can transform anticipated profits into losses.

Despite the experience, some traders remain vulnerable to these emotional responses. Financial markets, with their inherent volatility, intensify stress and magnify emotional responses. The innate human response to potential dangers or rewards can lead to decisions driven by fear or hope.

Mitigating these emotional responses involves multiple strategies. One way is diversifying an options portfolio, which can mitigate fear associated with losses in a specific sector. For instance, the impact is direct if a portfolio solely focuses on technology and that sector declines. By diversifying into areas like commodities or healthcare, losses in one sector may be cushioned by stability or gains in another.

Applying a range of options strategies can provide safeguards against fluctuating markets. Engaging in various trades, including calls, puts, long positions, or short positions, prepares traders for multiple market trajectories and offers stability during market downturns.

Clear guidelines before trading are necessary. Outline risk parameters for every trade. Set profit objectives and develop exit strategies for diverse market outcomes. Such predetermined guidelines can prevent decisions propelled by emotions.

Regularly assessing trading activity, encompassing profitable and loss-making trades, provides insights. Identifying recurring patterns in trading behavior, whether from hesitation due to fear or overconfidence from greed, informs better decision-making in subsequent trades.

Overcoming Emotional Biases

Emotional biases often drive traders away from logical decisions, prompting actions not in harmony with their set objectives or risk parameters.

Confirmation bias stands out prominently. Like everyone else, traders lean towards data that resonates with their pre-existing convictions. Take, for example, a trader optimistic about a stock; they may primarily pay heed to its favorable updates, sidelining any adverse indicators. This tunnel vision can distort a trader's market view and pave the way for imprudent decisions.

Equally pervasive is the ***loss aversion bias***. The distress associated with financial setbacks frequently overshadows the satisfaction from gains. This imbalance can entrap traders, making them cling to detrimental positions in hopes of a market reversal. Alternatively, the dread of potential losses might prompt premature exits from profitable positions.

Success breeds confidence, but excess of it begets overconfidence. Riding the wave of consecutive trading triumphs can inflate a trader's self-assessment. Such inflated self-belief can sometimes overshadow meticulous analysis, increasing susceptibility to hasty, high-risk decisions.

Combating these biases necessitates proactive measures. Identifying and understanding these predispositions offers a foundation. To counter confirmation bias, actively challenge your judgments, diversify information sources, and attempt to adopt varied market viewpoints.

Loss aversion can be addressed by instituting strict stop-loss orders. Before venturing into a trade, defining acceptable loss thresholds and adhering to them safeguards against emotion-driven choices.

Addressing overconfidence calls for introspection. A trading journal serves as a mirror, reflecting a trader's decisions, reasoning, and consequences. Periodic evaluation of this record provides a reality check, spotlighting areas needing attention and ensuring a balanced self-view.

The Importance of Patience in Trading

In trading, impatience often emerges as a bad trait, leading to rash decisions like taking unwarranted trades or cutting off successful ones. Cultivating patience is essential for upholding ideal trading discipline.

The roots of impatience can be traced back to several sources. ***Experiencing losses,*** especially after unsuccessful trades, can ignite the urge to recover. When market activity is minimal, ***boredom*** might attract you to engage excessively. A ***winning streak*** can also spark impatience, as you may search for their next opportunity hurriedly.

Impatience signifies a waning trust in one's trading approach. This can result in a departure from an established strategy, as traders may prioritize short-term gains over their standard criteria for promising setups. To foster patience, ***have an unwavering belief*** *in one's trading edge*. Analyzing previous trades can be insightful, offering a glimpse into how positive outcomes evolve over an extended period.

With a strong belief in your strategy, you cultivate the patience to wait for specific entry points, avoiding hasty decisions. Avoid cutting off profitable trades too early or delaying exits on less favorable ones. Exercising patience can sometimes mean enduring temporary setbacks to achieve lasting success.

During quieter trading intervals, ***remain proactive.*** Engage with market analyses, delve into books, revisit older trades, and envision future triumphs. Organize a list of potential opportunities to keep preparedness levels high and sidestep diversions during active trading hours. Maintaining a sense of progression can enhance patience.

Incorporate patience also into daily routines. Avoid rushing through tasks or making hasty decisions outside the trading realm. Designate time for calming activities and integrate regular exercise into routines to alleviate anxiety. Cultivating patience in daily life can seamlessly translate into trading practices.

Over time, as you gain experience and become more familiar with the market, patience naturally evolves. The broader strategy's potential outcomes become more apparent, overshadowing temporary setbacks. Singular losses no longer instigate impatience. Instead, traders focus on the broader perspective of each trade.

Developing a Trading Plan

Creating and implementing a detailed trading plan is essential for maintaining focus, discipline, and risk management in options trading. This plan should outline every aspect of your trading strategy and processes.

The Components of a Trading Plan

A clear definition of your market niche and the strategies you intend to implement should be at the core of your plan. **Determine the specific underlying securities** you plan to trade: *stocks, ETFs, indexes, or futures options.* Trace your overarching trading direction—encompassing strategies like trend following, mean reversion, spreads, or non-directional approaches.

Craft detailed entry rules that dictate when to consider a trade. Begin long calls when a stock price exceeds its 20-day moving average or set up a put credit spread when the implied volatility rank surpasses the 40th percentile. Clearly defined entry parameters are crucial.

The *exit rules* are equally vital, highlighting profitable exits and loss containment guidelines. Establish a specific profit target for closing positions and delineate rules for minimizing losses, such as exiting if the option premium is reduced by 50%. Implementing stop losses based on the percentage of capital at risk is imperative.

Detail your approach for selecting specific options trades, factoring in elements like strike price, expiration date, and the number of contracts with the account size and risk preferences. The criteria for selecting these components should be consistent with the expected direction and duration of the trade.

Incorporate solid risk management principles to mitigate emotional decisions. Define your risk parameters for each trade, considering your account size. Set firm boundaries for position size, maximum permissible loss for each trade, daily loss limits, and overall tolerances for account drawdown. Consistent adherence to these guidelines is essential.

Besides strategy, ensure that the plan includes *procedural elements.* This covers methods for assessing potential trades, the mechanics of placing orders, keeping records, and your commitment to continuous learning. A well-defined plan clarifies every trading aspect, instilling the discipline needed to trade in alignment with the outlined strategies and ensuring confidence in your approach.

Following the Plan

Trade executions should only occur when your plan's specific entry criteria come to fruition. Avoiding trades driven by impatience or recovering from prior losses is essential. Remember: *sidestep when a trade does not fit the specified guidelines, irrespective of any intuitive appeal.* Patience remains instrumental in awaiting ideal trading opportunities.

*Incorporate stop losses i*n all positions, as stipulated in your plan. This strategy safeguards capital; hence, refrain from making alterations due to emotions like fear or hope. Equally essential is to maintain consistency in position sizing. Even with an augmenting account balance, abide by the designated percentage boundaries for every trade.

Once trades are active, *resist the urge to modify positions constantly*. Avoid unnecessary adjustments and ensure that trades run their course, following your plan's stipulated rules. Concentrate solely on prospective trades that meet your entry prerequisites, avoiding excessive trading.

As positions approach their closure, *follow your plan*, adhering to pre-established profit targets and stop loss rules. It is unwise to prolong the duration of underperforming trades in anticipation of a revival. Avoid lingering also on profitable trades, aiming for disproportionate gains. Discipline during exits often translates to consistent success.

Before undertaking any trade, ***dedicate time to comprehensive analysis,*** following the systematic approach dictated by your plan. Rushing decisions can be detrimental. Order placements should align with your plan's mechanisms, such as employing limit orders to mitigate potential losses. Ensure your actions consistently reflect your outlined processes.

Conclude by ***revisiting your trading plan*** routinely before every trading session. Doing so serves as a refresher, solidifying discipline and assimilating the guidelines. Every trading choice should resonate with the plan's directives, sidelining emotional impulses. Adhering to your established trading framework cultivates a bias-free, clear-headed trading environment.

Review and Adjustments

Regularly examining your options trading plan and trade records is essential for process optimization. Markets transform; thus, while the essence of your strategy should be stable, its details need responsiveness to shifts.

Establish a routine for evaluations on a monthly or quarterly basis. Analyze your recent trades, delving into profit percentages, win rates, reward-to-risk ratios, and significant losses. Pinpoint trades or decisions that ranged from your original plan due to emotional influences.

Underperformance of specific trades, rules, or strategies might necessitate revisions. But caution is advised to prevent adjustments purely based on recent market dynamics. ***Validate any tweaks*** with a more extensive statistical backtest to ensure consistent advantages.

Opt for measurable indicators per your market philosophy in refining entry and exit parameters. For instance, a trader who follows trends might specify that trades only initiate when the ADX trend strength indicator crosses a specified level. Adjustments resonate with your foundational strategy.

Significant drops in your win rate or profit percentages should prompt a re-evaluation of risk protocols. Adjusting stop-loss points, recalibrating position sizes, or decreasing loss ceilings might be the answer before recalibrating the core strategy. Often, signs of risk management lapses precede a diminished strategy advantage. *Safeguarding capital* is vital.

When implementing changes, *record the updated guidelines in your plan.* Monitor these trades distinctly in the future. Refrain from incorporating numerous alterations at once. Dedicate time to measure the outcomes of one change before layering another. Verifying the effectiveness of adjustments demands patience.

The primary objective is refining your edge, not overhauling the strategy entirely. Even strong strategies face challenging phases. Abstain from radical shifts, placing more emphasis on selecting assets, managing risks, and planning trades. Adherence to your market segment is necessary.

Consistently maintain a thorough record of trades, thought processes, and strategies. Detailed data sets the stage for meaningful evaluations. A trading journal that captures trades, emotions, and plan deviations is invaluable. Self-reflection without bias is required.

Maintaining Discipline in Trading

With discipline, you can adopt a systematic, step-by-step approach to your trades. This structured method can increase your chances of success in the trading world.

Discipline in Trading Success

Establishing a trading discipline sustained success in options trading. This discipline requires persistent adherence to the trading strategy, even amid tumultuous market conditions or personal stressors. Such discipline ensures decisions are grounded in rationality and probability rather than being swayed by fleeting emotions like fear or greed.

In trading, discipline entails having unwavering trust and patience with your strategy, ensuring only opportunities meeting specific criteria are pursued. A disciplined trader maintains composure, even when trades turn off the anticipated path. Instead of making impulsive decisions or seeking unattainable profits, you stay the course if the market conditions diverge from your predefined criteria. Your vision is rooted in long-term achievements, not short-lived fluctuations.

Discipline naturally steers you from common pitfalls, including excessive trading, disproportionate risk-taking, or weakening guidelines. For example, a disciplined trader stays within predefined boundaries, willingly accepting marginal losses when required and prioritizing capital preservation over hoping for a trade reversal.

When faced with profitable scenarios, exercise restraint. Remain committed to your foundational strategy, ensuring you capitalize on your profits. Every trade undergoes an objective review to determine its alignment with the initial plan and acceptable risk parameters. The trajectory of a single trade does not dictate choices; a more expansive strategy does.

Continuous assessment and refinement of the trading strategy are integral to discipline. This process involves careful documentation of all trades, favorable or otherwise, to facilitate iterative learning and strategy optimization. The essence of discipline transcends mere profit generation; it emphasizes ongoing skill enhancement and trading mastery, drawing insights from every trade.

Once you cultivate and uphold discipline, you recognize that triumphs are a product of a dedicated approach. Over an extended timeline, fortified with a strong trading strategy, this unwavering and methodical approach paves the way for commendable returns and trading success.

Techniques for Improving Trading Discipline

Building and maintaining discipline in trading is a continuous journey, but you can enhance your discipline over time with the right techniques, including the following:

- **Self-awareness and Identification.** Begin by recognizing areas of weakened discipline, such as impulse trades, disregarding stop-loss points, aggressive loss recovery, or deviation from trading plans. Once recognized, establish specific rules to combat these tendencies. For example:
  - Cap the number of trades within a set period.
  - Limit trading to certain market conditions.
- **Structured Trading Routine.** Allocate specific hours solely for trading. Maintain strict adherence to pre-set entry and exit criteria. Designate set times to review potential trades. Employ tools like trade triggers and checklists to methodize the trading process.

- **Use of Stop Orders.** Implement stop orders instead of market orders to respect pre-decided exit points and curtail mid-trade hesitations.
- **Experiment with Caution.** When attempting a new trading strategy, commence with smaller trades. This minimizes risk and deters rash decisions prompted by the fear of substantial losses.
- **Maintain a Trading Journal.** Rigorously document trades, outcomes, emotions, and market analysis. Regularly review the journal to discern patterns, refine strategies, and enhance self-awareness.
- **Choose the Right Trading Circle.** Engage with experienced and disciplined traders for insights, objectivity, and accountability. Be discerning about the company; undisciplined traders can inadvertently endorse poor habits.
- **Adopt a Marathon Mentality.** Focus on consistent, strategic decision-making rather than individual wins or losses. Prioritize long-term strategy adherence over short-term results. Acknowledge that consistent strategy application over time will likely yield favorable outcomes.

The Importance of a Balanced Lifestyle

The pressures and stresses of trading can drain your mental bandwidth for disciplined decision-making over time. A balanced lifestyle provides stability for consistently executing your edge. To do so, do the following:

- **Establish clear boundaries between trading and personal life.** Engage in activities outside the market realm and refrain from checking positions outside trading hours. Cultivate relationships for a well-rounded perspective.
- **Prioritize physical health.** Commit to a balanced diet, regular exercise routines, and adequate sleep. A healthy

body supports mental sharpness and emotional stability during trading sessions.
- **Ensure sound personal finance management.** Avoid taking undue risks with non-trading assets and fund trading activities with savings instead of loans. A stable financial position minimizes external stresses that might interfere with trading decisions.
- **Engage with mentors and trading communities.** Their insights and experiences provide valuable guidance, especially during challenging phases. Understand that mastery in trading is a journey, and consistent efforts lead to gradual improvements.
- **Stay vigilant to signs of burnout, such as reduced motivation, diminished creativity, or deteriorating performance.** When these symptoms emerge, consider taking breaks to mentally and emotionally reset.

Emphasize overall well-being to ensure sustained energy and focus for effective trading implementation.

Chapter 8
Regulatory and Legal Aspects

Options trading is subject to laws and regulations enforced by government agencies to promote fair and orderly markets. This chapter examines the major regulatory bodies overseeing options trading, their role in establishing rules and protecting traders, and key regulations every trader should understand. Also covered are legal considerations around compliance, consequences of violations, and the importance of ethics in options trading to align with the spirit of regulations, foster market integrity, and build public trust.

Regulatory Bodies and Their Roles

In the U.S., the Securities and Exchange Commission and Financial Industry Regulatory Authority are key regulators overseeing options markets and brokerages. Traders can operate legally by understanding regulations like *risk disclosure, margin rules, reporting procedures,* and *position limits.* Regulatory oversight of options fosters fair, transparent markets and protects traders from misconduct.

Major Regulatory Bodies in Options Trading

There are several key regulatory agencies and organizations that govern the options trading industry in the United States. As an options trader, it is imperative to understand the role of each of these bodies in establishing rules, enforcing regulations, and protecting market participants.

The ***Securities and Exchange Commission (SEC)*** is the primary regulator for options trading markets. The SEC oversees options exchanges like the *Chicago Board Options Exchange (CBOE)* and brokers and dealers that trade or facilitate options trades. The SEC aims to ensure fair markets and trading practices, overseeing activities like order handling and execution, short selling, market manipulation, and insider trading involving options. They can suspend or ban brokers or traders for violations.

The ***Financial Industry Regulatory Authority (FINRA)*** is an independent organization authorized by Congress to protect investors and oversee broker-dealers. While the SEC has high-level market oversight, FINRA more narrowly regulates member brokerage firms and exchange members involved in options trading. FINRA enforces just and equitable trading regulations, registration requirements, due diligence, supervision, training, and arbitration. Violations can lead to censures, fines, or suspensions.

Another regulatory body is the ***Commodity Futures Trading Commission (CFTC)*** which focuses on the futures and commodities markets. They regulate options on futures and commodities, like S&P 500 futures options and crude oil options traded on the *Chicago Mercantile Exchange (CME)*. The CFTC governs registration, reporting, position limits, margin requirements, and other standards for futures options trading.

State securities regulators further supplement federal agencies with oversight of brokers and advisors operating within their states. The ***North American Securities Administrators Association (NASAA)*** coordinates state regulatory efforts on options trading. State rules may impose additional requirements beyond federal regulations.

Knowing these major regulators of options markets, exchanges, brokers, advisors, and traders enables comprehending applicable rules and operating legally.

The Role of Regulatory Bodies

Various government agencies overseeing options markets and brokers play a role in safeguarding traders' interests in several key ways.

Regulatory requirements **ensure the financial stability** of brokers and clearing houses to prevent disruptions for traders. Regulators impose capital, margin, and collateral requirements to minimize insolvency risks. Audits and oversight prevent fraud like the commingling of client and firm funds. Prudent regulation preserves market infrastructure integrity.

Regulators also **mandate extensive disclosure and transparency** from brokers to traders regarding trading risks, fees, compensation methods, and advisors' qualifications. This arms traders with information to evaluate risks and make informed decisions. Advertising rules prohibit misleading marketing claims.

Conduct standards enforced by regulators require brokers to act in clients' best interest, providing suitable recommendations aligned with their experience, risk appetite, and objectives. Supervision and compliance procedures must be in place to prevent abuse. Rules prohibit practices like front-running client trades.

Strict supervision of exchanges **enhances orderly markets free of manipulation**. Regulators monitor for abusive short selling, insider trading, spoofing, and other tactics that could artificially distort prices and disadvantage traders. Enforcement actions punish misconduct.

For futures options, limits on speculative positions instituted by the CFTC *prevent concentration risks* from large traders moving markets. This curbs volatility that could hurt smaller traders. The SEC's fiduciary rule also requires brokers to disclose conflicts of interest.

Such regulatory oversights give traders confidence to participate in markets knowing commissions, fees, and order handling practices are reasonable and transparent. Regulations promote fairness and reduce risks. Prudent traders view regulation as critical protection rather than unnecessary bureaucracy.

Understanding Regulatory Rules and Guidelines

These rules, established by oversight agencies, ensure that trading is conducted legally, ethically, and transparently. For options traders, understanding these regulations is not just a matter of compliance but also a means to make informed and strategic decisions. Some rules and requirements you should comprehend include:

- **Pattern Day Trading Rules.** The *Financial Industry Regulatory Authority (FINRA)* has established rules to curb excessive speculation, especially among traders with limited capital. Specifically, pattern day traders with less than $25,000 in equity are restricted in their trading activities. They can only trade options or stocks in a margin account if their balance exceeds the trade amount. This rule is designed to prevent traders from taking undue risk and incurring significant losses they cannot cover.
- **SEC Options Disclosure Document (ODD).** Before diving into options trading, traders must familiarize themselves with the *Options Disclosure Document (ODD)*. This document, mandated by the *Securities and Exchange Commission (SEC)*, outlines the various risks associated with options trading. These risks range from the potential for

unlimited losses to the complexities inherent in certain options strategies. The ODD is a comprehensive guide, ensuring traders know what they are getting into.

- **Position Limits.** To maintain market integrity and prevent potential manipulation, the SEC and the *Commodity Futures Trading Commission (CFTC)* have set limits on the maximum number of options contract positions a trader can hold. These limits vary depending on the type and class of the underlying asset. Awareness of these limits is crucial to ensure compliance and strategize trades effectively.
- **Exercise Settlement Procedures.** Certain obligations come into play when an option expires, especially for option writers. Traders need to understand the procedures surrounding the exercise and settlement of options. This knowledge ensures that traders fulfill their obligations and avoid potential violations.
- **Margin Requirements.** Margin trading allows traders to borrow money from their broker to purchase securities. Brokers, however, require traders to maintain a certain margin to cover potential losses on options trades. The required margin varies depending on the risk associated with each position. Understanding margin requirements is vital to manage risk and prevent potential defaults.
- **Expiration Dates and Times.** All options have a pre-determined expiration date and time, typically on Saturday mornings. Attempting to exercise an option outside of these parameters can lead to complications. Being aware of expiration procedures ensures smooth trading operations.
- **Do Not Call List.** FINRA has established a *"Do Not Call"* list to protect traders from unsolicited and high-pressure sales tactics. Traders can opt into this list to avoid unwanted calls from brokers, ensuring a more peaceful trading experience.

- Trade Reporting. Accurate record-keeping is not just good practice; it is a legal requirement. Traders must report their gains and losses accurately and promptly for tax purposes. Underreporting or misreporting can lead to legal repercussions.
- **Anti-Money Laundering Rules.** To combat illegal activities and ensure the financial system's integrity, brokers must identify their traders and report any suspicious activities. This means traders should always operate their accounts under their true legal names and be transparent in their transactions.
- **Categories of Options Traders.** Different traders have different needs, and brokers recognize this by categorizing customers into institutional, professional, and retail groups. Each category comes with its own set of protections and requirements. Knowing where you fit in can help you navigate the trading landscape more effectively.

Beyond the technicalities and specifics, the spirit of these regulations is clear: *to ensure fairness, transparency, and protection for all market participants.*

Legal Considerations

Violating options trading compliance requirements can result in significant fines, license suspensions, enforced position reductions, and even criminal prosecution in egregious fraud cases. To trade ethically and successfully, try to educate themselves on relevant regulations and legal obligations.

Legal Aspects of Options Trading

Like any other financial instrument, options trading operates within a framework of laws and regulations, such as:

- **Contractual Nature of Options.** An option is a contract that holds both parties involved—*the buyer and the seller*—to have specific rights and obligations. Understanding these rights and obligations is the first step in navigating the legal landscape of options trading.
- **Standardized Contracts.** Unlike custom contracts in other forms of trading, option contracts are standardized in terms of contract size, expiration date, strike price, and other terms. The options exchanges enforce this standardization and ensure that every option contract of a particular type and strike price is identical to every other, making them tradable in the open market.
- **Regulation of Options Exchanges.** These exchanges have rules and regulations that members must follow, ensuring that trading is orderly and that traders are protected from fraudulent activities. For instance, the exchanges have mechanisms to ensure that the prices at which trades are executed are fair and reflect the market conditions.
- **Disclosure Requirements.** Option sellers must disclose specific information to potential buyers, especially those who write options. This includes details about the underlying asset, the strike price, the expiration date, and other relevant information. Doing so ensures the buyer has all the necessary information to make an informed decision.
- **Settlement and Clearing.** The legal framework also covers the settlement of option contracts. When an option is exercised, the contract is settled, meaning the underlying asset is transferred from the seller to the buyer or from the buyer to the seller. Clearinghouses, regulated entities that stand between the two parties in

a trade, ensure that this process is smooth and that both parties fulfill their obligations.
- **Margin Requirements.** To trade options, traders might be required to maintain a margin account, especially if they are writing options. This is a type of account where the trader deposits a certain amount of money or securities as collateral. The legal framework dictates the minimum margin requirements and their calculation, ensuring traders have enough capital to cover potential losses.

As a trader, understanding these legalities is about compliance and ensuring you are well-positioned to protect your investments and trade. As you continue your journey in options trading, always keep these legal considerations at the forefront of your strategy.

The Importance of Compliance

Though different brokers have specific rules, there are overarching regulations mandated by financial regulatory bodies that you must follow irrespective of your broker. Familiarize yourself with SEC and FINRA guidelines on options trading to avoid inadvertent violations.

Some key compliance aspects to focus on include:

- **Trade Disclosure Rules.** SEC and FINRA have strict regulations requiring the clear declaration of any vested interests in proposed trades. Traders must also provide thorough details regarding past performances. Make it a point to share information about your qualifications, the potential risks in your trading strategies, and an exhaustive breakdown of performance metrics.
- **Account Approvals.** Before clients can engage in certain options trading strategies, brokers need to approve their accounts. This approval hinges on the clients' trading

history and financial standing. Providing accurate details about your qualifications and strictly sticking to trades within the approved parameters is necessary as a trader.
- **Position Limits.** Regulatory bodies, such as the CBOE, set limits on the maximum number of open contract positions that a trader can hold. These limits are set to deter any potential market manipulation. Familiarize yourself with these limits for each class of options to ensure compliance.
- **Insider Trading.** Engaging in trades based on privileged, non-public information that offers an unfair trading advantage is unethical and illegal.
- **Record-keeping.** For tax purposes and by IRS guidelines, you should diligently maintain comprehensive records of all your trading activities. Preserve essential documents, including but not limited to *account statements, trade confirmations,* and *trading-related communications.*
- **Regulation SHO.** Adherence to SEC's directives on short selling is non-negotiable. These directives encompass requirements such as compulsory borrowing before initiating a short and addressing failure to deliver.
- **Options Disclosure Document.** Brokers furnish an Options Disclosure Document (ODD) that elucidates the risks and characteristics associated with options. Review and acknowledge this document, as your signature on the ODD is a prerequisite to start trading options.

Lack of compliance can destroy your finances, reputation, and freedom if you get into legal trouble. Consult a trading attorney if needed to strengthen compliance. Partnering with a reputable broker also helps ensure you stay compliant. With vigilance and knowledge of rules, compliance can become a healthy habit that keeps your options trading legitimate.

Legal Consequences of Non-Compliance

The potential repercussions of non-compliance are the following:

- **Financial Penalties.** Financial penalties are one of the most immediate consequences of non-compliance in options trading. Regulatory bodies can impose hefty fines on traders and institutions that violate trading rules. These fines range from relatively minor amounts for small infractions to substantial sums for more egregious violations. For instance, failing to meet margin requirements or engaging in manipulative trading practices can result in significant financial penalties.
- **Suspension or Revocation of Trading Privileges.** Regulatory bodies and exchanges take non-compliance seriously. Traders who violate trading rules repeatedly may find their trading privileges suspended or permanently revoked. This means they would be prohibited from executing trades on specific exchanges or across multiple platforms. For professional traders and institutions, this can be a career-ending consequence.
- **Legal Proceedings.** In cases where non-compliance is suspected of being part of a larger fraudulent scheme or involves criminal activities, legal proceedings may be initiated. This could lead to a lengthy court battle, with potential outcomes ranging from acquittal to imprisonment, depending on the severity of the violation and the jurisdiction in which the case is tried.
- **Reputational Damage.** In finance and trading, reputation is vital. Non-compliance, especially when it leads to publicized legal battles or significant financial penalties, can tarnish a trader's or institution's reputation. This can result in lost business opportunities, strained relationships with other market participants, and a general loss of trust in the trading community.

- **Restitution to Affected Parties.** In some cases, non-compliance can result in financial harm to other market participants. When this occurs, regulatory bodies may require the offending party to make restitution. This means compensating those who suffered financial losses due to the non-compliant actions. Restitution can be in addition to any financial penalties imposed by regulatory bodies.
- **Increased Scrutiny.** Even if a trader or institution is not immediately penalized for non-compliance, they may come under increased scrutiny from regulatory bodies. This heightened oversight can make trading more challenging, as regulators may closely monitor all trading activities to ensure compliance. This can lead to increased operational costs and potential delays in executing trades.
- **Mandatory Training or Education.** In some instances, especially for minor infractions, regulatory bodies may require traders or institutions to undergo mandatory training or education. This ensures that the offending party fully understands the rules and regulations governing options trading and is less likely to commit further violations.

Non-compliance is never worth the temporary profits you may make illegally in options trading. Stay current on rule changes, maintain detailed records, disclose everything, and consult experts to avoid compliance missteps. While perfection is impossible, striving to trade ethically within laws will help you sleep better and trade longer without unwanted legal disasters.

Ethical Trading Practices

Trading ethically is key for long-term success in options trading. While regulations set legal standards, ethical principles go beyond rules. Ethics involve transparency, integrity, client focus, truthfulness about risks, and avoiding conflicts of interest. Unethical conduct may bring temporary gains but destroys reputations when unacceptable practices surface. Always establish an ethical foundation that promotes transparent, client-centric trading to sustain trust and success.

The Importance of Ethics in Trading

The financial market's very foundation is trust. Traders enter the market believing that it will operate efficiently, that their counterparts will act in good faith, and that the data they base their decisions on is accurate. This trust is nurtured and fortified by ethical trading practices. When you consistently act with integrity, you not only protect their reputation but also contribute to a market environment that is transparent and reliable, benefiting all stakeholders.

Ethical trading is pivotal in safeguarding investors, especially those who might be venturing into the market for the first time or with limited knowledge. The market is rife with opportunities, but it also presents pitfalls, some resulting from unethical behaviors like *disseminating misleading information* or *deploying manipulative trading tactics*. Such actions can lead unsuspecting investors astray, resulting in significant financial setbacks and diminished faith in the trading ecosystem.

While some might argue that bending the rules can lead to quick gains, such a strategy is myopic. Short-term wins achieved through dubious means are unsustainable and can lead to severe repercussions, both legally and reputationally. In contrast, traders who embed ethical considerations into their strategies often find that they can cultivate lasting business relationships, enjoy sustained success, and position themselves as respected figures in the trading community.

Beyond the tangible benefits and potential pitfalls, ethical trading also *reflects a trader's personal integrity.* There is an intrinsic value in knowing that one's actions are upright and just. This internal compass not only guides traders through complex decisions but also offers a sense of fulfillment that transcends monetary gains. Every trade and every decision has ripple effects, and acting ethically ensures that their impact on the broader market and society is positive.

Another often overlooked aspect of ethical trading is its *role in mitigating systemic risks.* Practices that skew the market's natural dynamics can introduce vulnerabilities into the financial system. These distortions, if widespread, can trigger cascading effects, potentially destabilizing broader economic structures. Ethical trading acts as a bulwark against such risks, ensuring that the market remains robust and resilient.

An ethical trading environment is fertile ground for innovation and growth. A transparent and fair market draws diverse participants, enhancing liquidity and opening doors to novel trading strategies, products, and technologies. This influx of ideas and approaches can propel the entire industry forward, creating value for all involved.

Common Unethical Practices in Trading

Understanding common unethical practices ensures your activities remain above board and contribute positively to the market's integrity.

- **Front Running.** Occurs when traders execute orders based on privileged knowledge of forthcoming orders from clients or the general market. By capitalizing on this information before its widespread release, they obtain an

advantageous position, often compromising other market participants.
- **Churning.** A broker engages in excessive buying and selling in a client's account, driven to gain commissions rather than serve the client's best interests. This behavior can lessen the client's trust and cause substantial financial liability.
- **Wash Trading.** Traders concurrently buy and sell identical financial instruments to create false, artificial market activity. This tactic can falsely project an amplified interest or liquidity in a specific asset, potentially skewing its market value.
- **Insider Trading.** This malpractice sees traders leveraging material information about a security that is not available to the public. Such actions give the trader an undue edge, tarnishing the market's transparency.
- **Quote Stuffing.** Traders rapidly submit and retract many orders, inundating the market with data. The primary objective is to disorient or decelerate competing traders or automated systems, enabling the unethical trader to benefit from possible price discrepancies.
- **Pump and Dump.** Traders artificially escalate the price of an asset *(the "pump")* via the propagation of deceptive positive information. Following the price augmentation, they offload their positions *(the "dump")*, resulting in a swift price downturn and inflicting losses on those lured during the inflated phase.
- **Spoofing.** Large orders are placed with zero intent of finalization. The underlying objective is to deceive other traders about an asset's supply or demand, causing price alterations beneficial to the spoofer, which then exploits the resultant price movement.
- **Misrepresentation.** Covers a spectrum from brokers disseminating false details about investment commodities to traders circulating baseless rumors about enterprises.

These maneuvers can misguide investors, compelling them to act on deceptive information.
- **Overleveraging.** While leverage can boost gains, its excessive use without proper risk communication to clients is considered unethical. Such actions can precipitate vast losses, especially amidst unpredictable markets.
- **Ignoring Conflict of Interest.** At times, brokers or traders might possess interests at odds with their clients. Proceeding on these interests without proper disclosure is unethical and can engender client distrust and financial jeopardy.

Adopting options trading practices that prioritize self-gain over client welfare breaches ethical principles. Upholding transparency and honesty and placing client interests at the forefront are vital. Failure to adhere to ethical practices will inevitably lead to accountability by clients and regulatory bodies.

Promoting Ethical Trading Practices

As an options trader, you must uphold ethical trading practices. Adhering to an ethical code of conduct will not only keep you on the right side of regulations but also promote a healthy trading environment.

To begin with, ***make truthful representations*** about your qualifications, capabilities, and past performance as a trader. Do not overstate your skills or misrepresent your track record to attract clients or investors. Be transparent about your background, investment style, and risk management strategies. When you have limited experience, be upfront about it rather than pretending to be an expert.

When executing trades, ***exercise due diligence*** to avoid misleading counterparties. Disclose any potential conflicts of interest you may have, such as existing positions in the underlying asset. Provide accurate information about the traded securities so the counterparty can make informed decisions. Refrain from making false statements or withholding material facts.

In your trading activities, ***avoid practices like front running, churning, pumping, and dumping.*** These undermine market integrity and could have legal consequences. Trade ethically without such deceptive tactics.

Handle your clients' capital as responsibly as your own. Make investment decisions aligned with their goals and risk appetite, not yours. Be prudent in taking risks with their funds. Disclose the risks involved and do not misrepresent potential outcomes. Avoid overpromising unrealistic returns. Your duty is to grow their capital sustainably.

When things go wrong, ***take responsibility for your actions*** instead of looking to blame others. As you made a poor judgment call, acknowledge it, learn from it, and improve. Do not try to cover up mistakes or pass the buck. Admitting errors shows integrity and prevents repeating the same mistakes.

Compete vigorously as a trader, but avoid malicious practices like spreading false rumors or manipulating prices. Compete based on superior insights and execution, not by undermining others. A healthy competitive spirit that spurs innovation is good, while cutthroat competition harms the ecosystem.

Keep improving your knowledge of ethical regulations and industry best practices. Stay updated on policies related to insider trading, short selling, speculation limits, and other aspects. Know where to draw the line between astute trading and unethical behavior. If in doubt, seek advice from compliance experts.

Adopting ethical trading practices requires discipline, especially when others around you may be cutting corners. But you will gain a reputation for being a principled trader who succeeds through merit rather than malpractice. When you trade ethically, you promote fair markets, build relationships, and sleep better at night.

Chapter 9
Building a Successful Career

Achieving long-term success as an options trader requires dedication to continually learning, adapting your strategies, and balancing trading with your personal life. This chapter provides essential tips for developing good routines, managing stress, and pursuing interests outside trading.

Developing a Consistent Trading Routine

Establishing a solid daily routine includes planning your trading sessions, reviewing the markets, and analyzing trades.

The Importance of a Consistent Routine

Having structure and repeating the same habits minimizes emotion-driven decisions and reinforces professional trading behaviors. When you implement your process systematically day after day, you are much less likely to make impulsive trades that deviate from your plan.

Your daily routine should include scheduled steps like *reviewing your watchlist, scanning for significant news events or earnings, checking economic data, analyzing charts to identify potential trades, clearly defining entries and exits for ideas, managing open positions, booking profits and losses,* and *reviewing your overall performance at the end of each day.* Performing these tasks methodically helps detect patterns in your trading and markets, allowing refinements over time.

Approaching options trading with discipline and structure *establishes solid habits and skills* that set you up for long-term consistency. Trades should be made as part of your defined routine, not based on emotions or outside your system. A sense of orderly flow from step to step prevents you from skipping or rushing important actions in the process.

Psychologically, a consistent routine also *contributes to a professional, business-minded mentality* that serves you well. Treat options trading like a business you are developing - with set working hours, scheduled tasks, daily observation of processes, and analysis of performance data. This orderly attitude minimizes careless mistakes while maximizing learning.

Having specific checklists and procedures mapped out to follow in various market conditions will *help cement confidence in your abilities* over time as you master your craft through repetition. Tweak and refine the details of your routine gradually while maintaining the overall trading framework.

Creating a Daily Trading Routine

To create an effective daily trading routine, start by *setting regular working hours that align with your natural rhythms and open market.* Many successful active traders focus on the first 1 to 3 hours after the open, as this is often when the most opportunities emerge.

Make also a morning checklist of tasks to complete in 30 to 60 minutes, involving the following:

- Checking financial news sites for any significant events or announcements.
- Scanning overnight global market performance.
- Analyzing relevant economic data like employment figures.
- Reviewing charts, indicators, and patterns to identify potential trades.
- Defining specific entry and exit points in advance for trades
- Leave sufficient time before the opening to analyze information and think methodically about high-probability trades. Do not rush your preparation.

Once the market opens, *focus intently on executing your plan*. Look for defined trade triggers and criteria to be met before entering any trades. Execute entries and exits decisively based on your rules.

Set up position price and volume alerts to avoid sitting and monitor the screens all day. Schedule periodic also short breaks to clear your mind— *even 10 minutes away can boost productivity tremendously.*

Check in frequently on open positions and be prepared to take quick profits or cut losses based on your strategy. Do not let winners turn into losers or get married to a trade.

Make time at fixed intervals to comprehensively review your open positions, overall daily performance, and execution. Identify any deviations from your plan and improve.

End each day by ***logging all your trades*** with notes and analyzing the outcomes. Look for weaknesses in your process and any patterns or changes needed. Objectively review both gains and losses with a learning mentality.

In addition to your daily routine, *schedule longer-term reviews*. Analyze your overall performance metrics each week or month to assess what is working well and what needs refinement as market conditions change.

An options trader's work is never done— commit to lifelong skills development through repetition and analysis of your processes via scheduled routines. The market continuously evolves, so you must adapt and improve along with it. **Design a routine that optimizes your strengths as a trader.** Standardize as many elements as possible while leaving room to be adaptable. Turn options trading into a structured, professional pursuit via comprehensive daily habits and routines, building consistency and resilience over the long term.

Continuous Learning and Adaptation

Ongoing learning and adapting to evolving markets are essential to long-term success in options trading. Stay informed on market developments and be willing to refine your strategies.

The Importance of Continuous Learning

Markets are dynamic, so you cannot rigidly stick to the same approach at all times. For example, high volatility periods require closer monitoring of open positions and markets. You may need to place tighter stops or take profits faster when swift price swings could threaten open trades. Breaking news events also necessitate paying greater attention to markets to act decisively.

During slower, low-volatility periods, patience and discipline to avoid overtrading are necessary. Look for the best high-probability trade setups and be selective. Consider widening stops or reducing position sizes to lower risk. Reduce also trading frequency when markets are not conducive to your strategy. Wait for optimal conditions rather than force trades.

Continually review your performance metrics and find weaknesses in your process. Refine entry and exit criteria if you are struggling. Study market conditions and adjust your indicators or technical analysis methods as needed. The most successful traders evolve over time rather than rigidly stick to the same approach in all environments.

Adaptability, an open mindset, and a drive for improvement will serve you well throughout your trading career.

Keeping Up with Market Trends

From new trading platforms to changing regulations and market trends, keep up with all relevant developments to trade effectively. ***Monitor finance sites and blogs*** daily for news that could impact your existing strategies and uncover new opportunities.

Pay attention to new option products like weekly or mini options that may give you more flexibility. Understand shifts in market sentiment and rotation between sectors to identify where the trading edge may be at any time.

Follow quarterly earnings reports to understand how companies in your watchlist perform fundamentally. Keep up with mergers and acquisitions, which can greatly impact associated stocks.

Look for relatively underfollowed options with potential based on your analysis rather than sticking only to the most liquid products. Be willing to adapt your watchlist over time.

Track changes in regulations, tax laws, or rules that affect options trading. For example, adjustments to margin requirements can alter the capital required to trade certain strategies. Stay informed on all relevant financial and economic news that may directly or indirectly impact your trading.

Balancing Trading with Personal Life

Maintaining a work-life balance and pursuing personal interests is essential for sustaining a long career. Make time for relationships, health, and recreation outside of trading.

The Importance of Work-Life Balance

Dedicating oneself to trading can sometimes overshadow other vital aspects of life. Yet, striking a harmonious balance between work and personal life ensures longevity in an options trading career. The volatility and pressures of trading can exert a significant emotional toll if self-care falls by the wayside.

Allocating quality time for close family and friends is essential, irrespective of market behaviors or open positions. Prioritize physical well-being by maintaining a nutritious diet, following regular exercise routines, and ensuring restful sleep.

Given the emotionally charged nature of trading, burnout lurks around the corner. *Establish clear boundaries to ensure time for recovery and leisure.* Engage in hobbies that distract and revitalize the mind and soul.

Define yourself beyond trading metrics. Understand that personal worth extends beyond trading successes or failures. Nurturing diverse facets of life offers a safety net during challenging trading phases.

Surprisingly, a balanced life augments trading capabilities. A well-rested and multifaceted individual exhibits sharper focus, enhanced decision-making prowess, and resilience against trading-induced emotional disturbances.

Managing Stress and Burnout

The inherent uncertainties of trading always lead to stress, demanding proactive management strategies. Unaddressed, this stress can culminate in burnout, compromising mental and physical well-being.

Incorporate mindfulness and meditation into daily routines to neutralize trading-induced anxiety and promote clear-headed decision-making. A commitment to regular physical activity aids in stress alleviation.

Evaluate personal attitudes and beliefs about trading. Recognize and fix destructive psychological patterns, such as linking self-esteem solely to trading outcomes.

Engaging professional guidance, especially from trading psychologists, can be valuable. They equip traders with strategies to fortify their mental resilience.

Recognize the importance of breaks. If trading overshadows mental peace, health, or personal relationships, take time off to recalibrate. Prioritize well-being over fleeting market gains.

Pursuing Personal Interests and Hobbies

Enriching hobbies outside trading is pivotal for sustained trading enthusiasm and success. Such activities offer a sanctuary from market pressures, fostering holistic personal growth.

Designate regular intervals for activities and interactions free of trading influences. Engage in reading, athletic pursuits, arts, volunteering, or continuous learning.

Embarking on travels, local explorations, or international adventures provides a refreshing break from trading routines. Physical detachment from trading spaces can be invigorating.

Cultivate deep-rooted relationships through shared experiences with family and acquaintances. Resist the allure of an all-consuming trading existence.

Experiment with tactile skills like culinary arts, gardening, or visual arts. Creating something tangible offers a grounding experience.

For those inclined, engage in spiritual or religious practices. Such pursuits offer a perspective beyond the transient ebbs and flows of the market.

Above all, select activities that resonate on a personal level, offering genuine pleasure and relaxation. By immersing oneself wholeheartedly in these endeavors, one can harness their rejuvenating power.

Maintaining vibrant engagements outside the trading arena ensures a contented, balanced life, energizing traders for sustainable and fulfilling careers.

Conclusion

Reflecting upon the chapters, the starting point was grasping the fundamentals of what options represent and their role in financial markets. This led to exploring the intricate mechanics of options trading, shedding light on the nuances of initiating and concluding trades, and pinpointing indispensable tools for trading successes.

The guide continued with the three analysis pillars—*fundamental, technical, and sentiment*—to facilitate informed trading decisions. This foundation paved the way to unravel many trading strategies, ranging from the rudimentary, such as long calls and puts, to the intricate, like straddles, strangles, and iron condors.

Risk, a factor of trading, was examined. The multifaceted risks intrinsic to options trading were studied, revealing techniques to mitigate these inherent risks. A spotlight was also cast on diversification's pivotal role in carving a resilient trading portfolio.

Diving deeper, trading psychology and the quintessence of discipline emerged as cardinal topics. The emotional tribulations traders grapple with and the paramountcy of unwavering discipline in trading decisions became evident. This discourse was augmented by emphasizing the crafting of a robust trading plan and its rigorous adherence.

Navigating further, the discourse documented the regulatory and legal corridors of options trading. Recognizing regulatory body functions and the indispensability of legal adherence and ethical trading stood out. Culminating this voyage was a guide to forging a prosperous career in options trading, underlined by the imperatives of a steadfast trading routine, perpetual learning, and lifestyle equilibrium.

Options trading, while complex, unveils unparalleled rewards for those who conquer its intricacies. This guide has attempted to arm you with knowledge and tools grounded in real-world applicability and proven efficacy. Understanding that trading is personal and subjective is pivotal. Hence, the strategies explained herein must be tailored to your trading temperaments and fiscal aspirations.

Persistence, discipline, and patience are the beacons on the horizon of the trading journey. Trading victories are gradual, molded by relentless endeavor and ceaseless enlightenment. Though celebratory, every setback should be perceived as a lesson, and every triumph should be met with humility and reflection.

In essence, options trading is enriched with learning and evolution. It demands an unyielding grasp of market dynamics and an innate drive for growth. As this chapter concludes, this book indicates the birth of practical application, a phase where theory transforms into action.

Techniques Recap

The following are the techniques found in "Options Trading [All in 1]:

#	Technique/Hack	Explanation
1	Prompt Execution	To capitalize on favorable market conditions or minimize potential losses, traders must execute trades promptly.
2	Segmenting Trade Exits	Instead of attempting to exit a trade in its entirety instantaneously, dividing it into smaller segments for closure over time can prove advantageous.
3	Avoid Impulsive Trades	Resist impulsive actions, such as quickly selling or buying market-price options to terminate the trade.
4	Use Underlying Assets	Employ the underlying asset, be it a stock or an ETF, to conclude their positions. This involves executing transactions in the underlying entity to counterbalance the directional implications stemming from the options contracts.
5	Analyze Net Income Trends	Observing and analyzing the net income trends can offer predictive insights.
6	Monitor Corporate News	For an options trader, continuous vigilance over corporate news, comprehension of its implications, and strategic assimilation of such insights into trading decisions are indispensable. This necessitates regular monitoring of press releases, earnings announcements, and other conduits broadcasting corporate news.
7	Long Call Strategy	When deploying a long call, you can oversee a considerable quantity of shares with a minimal expense relative to outright stock acquisition. As these anticipations about the asset's price surge materialize, the ensuing returns could overshadow the preliminary expense linked to the option premium.
8	Capitalizing on Decline with Put Options	By purchasing a put option, you can capitalize on the declining price, and the deeper the asset's price dives below the option's strike price, the higher the potential profit.
9	Portfolio Safeguarding with Puts	Investors can safeguard their portfolios by purchasing put options on assets they already own or on broader market indices. If the market does decline, any losses incurred from the fall in the value of their stocks could be offset, at least in part, by the gains from their long put positions.

Options Trading [All-in-1]

#	Technique/ Hack	Explanation
10	Early Exercise of Puts	When the put option gains substantial value preceding its expiration, induced by a pronounced decline in the underlying asset's price, traders may opt for an early exercise or even sell the option to realize profits.
11	Delta for Position Sizing	Applying delta in trading can aid in position sizing. Traders can assess the potential change in their option's value for a given movement in the underlying asset and adjust their position based on risk tolerance.
12	Gamma Risk Assessment	For traders, gamma helps gauge the risk associated with their delta exposure. A rapidly changing delta could lead to higher potential profits and losses. By monitoring gamma, traders can understand how their risk profile might change as the underlying asset moves.
13	Vega in Volatility Analysis	If they expect volatility to increase, holding options with high positive Vega values might be beneficial. However, a sudden drop in IV can adversely impact these positions, highlighting the importance of using Vega for risk assessment.
14	Strategy Tweaking	Tweaking the strategy involves dealing with options that are deeper "in-the-money" or further "out-of-the-money." Consider time's impact on option values and the prevailing market uncertainty. Reduced market volatility might lead to diminished option premiums, warranting caution. Quick upward stock movements might necessitate strategic adjustments. Mastery over covered calls requires consistent practice.
15	Put Option Positioning	To adopt this position, secure the puts after obtaining the stock. Ensure the number of puts corresponds with the number of shares, with a single option corresponding to 100. Opt for a strike price mirroring the stock's prevailing price. Aligning the strike in this manner optimizes the put's value when the stock price decreases. Allocate complete cash reserves for the puts, sidestepping the use of margin, which could lead to unforeseen liquidation.
16	Analyzing Breakeven	Analyze the breakeven, including premiums received. Appropriate position sizing, stop losses, and spread widths help control risk.
17	Avoid Overpaying for Puts	Avoid overpaying for puts. Compare the put cost to just selling the stock and rebuying after a correction. Leverage your stock expertise to time trades well.
18	Risk-Reward Consideration	Weigh risk-reward carefully before trading. Contextualize the profit being capped versus premiums earned or hedging benefits obtained. Ensure adequate compensation for the defined risks. Containing risk means lost opportunity in exchange for greater certainty. Judge trades accordingly.
19	Call Option Selling Strategy	Selling a call option at an inferior strike price while buying another at a superior strike price limits the potential profit to the net premium received, adjusted by the difference between the two strike prices.

#	Technique/ Hack	Explanation
20	Timing in Long Straddle	The success of the long straddle often rests heavily on precise timing. Identifying signs or impending events that might induce significant price fluctuations in the underlying asset is needed.
21	Managing Exposure	Exposure. Allocating an overly generous portion of one's trading capital to a singular long straddle is inadvisable. Spreading investments across diverse strategies and underlying assets aids a more balanced risk management approach.
22	Choosing Extended Expiration Options	A common approach to countering this is opting for options with extended expiration, allowing sufficient room for desired market movements.
23	Precision in Butterfly Spread	Initiating a Butterfly Spread demands precision. Begin with selecting the right strike prices. As three are involved, their proximity to the current price and each other plays a role in determining the potential outcome. The spacing between these strikes can further influence the strategy's potential profit and loss, making it an essential factor to ponder.
24	Avoiding Overreliance on Past Success	Just because a particular setup has worked in the past does not guarantee future success. Always analyze each trade on its merit, and stay focused.
25	Managing Aggressive Market Movements	If the market starts moving aggressively against a position, closing out or adjusting the trade to manage risks might be wise.
26	Max Loss Determination	Before entering any trade, determine the maximum amount you could lose. For most options strategies, the maximum loss is the premium paid. However, the potential loss can be substantial for strategies like selling naked options. Always ensure that you are comfortable with the worst-case scenario.
27	Exit Strategy Planning	Always Have an Exit Strategy. Before entering any trade, know when and how you will exit. Be it taking profits at a certain level or cutting losses, having a clear exit strategy can help you manage risks effectively.
28	Counter Confirmation Bias	To counter confirmation bias, actively challenge your judgments, diversify information sources, and attempt to adopt varied market viewpoints.
29	Patience in Trade Management	Avoid cutting off profitable trades too early or delaying exits on less favorable ones. Exercising patience can sometimes mean enduring temporary setbacks to achieve lasting success.
30	Avoid Unnecessary Adjustments	Avoid unnecessary adjustments and ensure that trades run their course, following your plan's stipulated rules.

Options Trading [All-in-1]

#	Technique/Hack	Explanation
31	Effective Daily Trading Routine	To create an effective daily trading routine, start by setting regular working hours that align with your natural rhythms and open market. Many successful active traders focus on the first 1 to 3 hours after the open, as this is often when the most opportunities emerge.
32	Monitor Finance Sites and Blogs	Monitor finance sites and blogs daily for news that could impact your existing strategies and uncover new opportunities.
33	Establish Clear Boundaries	Establish clear boundaries to ensure time for recovery and leisure. Engage in hobbies that distract and revitalize the mind and soul.
34	Evaluate Personal Trading Attitudes	Evaluate personal attitudes and beliefs about trading. Recognize and fix destructive psychological patterns, such as linking self-esteem solely to trading outcomes.

References

Andersen, L., & Andreasen, J. (2000). Jump-diffusion processes: Volatility smile fitting and numerical methods for option pricing. Review of Derivatives Research, 4(3).

Augen, J. (2008). The volatility edge in options trading: New technical strategies for investing in unstable markets. FT Press.

Bakshi, G., Cao, C., & Chen, Z. (2000). Pricing and hedging long-term options. The Journal of Econometrics, 94(1-2).

Bates, D. S. (1996). Jumps and stochastic volatility: Exchange rate processes implicit in Deutsche Mark options. The Review of Financial Studies, 9(1).

Bates, D. S. (2000). Post-'87 crash fears in the S&P 500 futures option market. Journal of Econometrics, 94(1-2).

Black, F., & Scholes, M. (1973). The Pricing of Options and Corporate Liabilities. Journal of Political Economy, 81(3).

Broadie, M., & Detemple, J. (1996). American option valuation: New bounds, approximations, and a comparison of existing methods. The Review of Financial Studies, 9(4).

Carr, P., & Madan, D. (1999). Option valuation using the fast Fourier transform. Journal of Computational Finance, 2(4).

Carr, P., Geman, H., Madan, D. B., & Yor, M. (2002). The fine structure of asset returns: An empirical investigation. The Journal of Business, 75(2).

CBOE. (2018). CBOE Handbook of Option Strategies. Chicago Board Options Exchange.

Chance, D. M., & Brooks, R. (2015). Introduction to derivatives and risk management (10th ed.). Cengage Learning.

Chriss, N. A. (1996). Black-Scholes and beyond: Option pricing models. Irwin Professional Pub.

Cox, J. C., Ross, S. A., & Rubinstein, M. (1979). Option pricing: A simplified approach. Journal of Financial Economics, 7(3).

Derman, E., & Kani, I. (1994). Riding on a smile. RISK-London-RISK Magazine Limited, 7(2).

Dumas, B., Fleming, J., & Whaley, R. E. (1998). Implied volatility functions: Empirical tests. The Journal of Finance, 53(6).

Fouque, J. P., Papanicolaou, G., & Sircar, R. (2000). Derivatives in financial markets with stochastic volatility. Cambridge University Press.

Gatheral, J. (2006). The volatility surface: A practitioner's guide. John Wiley & Sons.

Geman, H., El Karoui, N., & Rochet, J. C. (1995). Changes of numéraire, changes of probability measure and option pricing. Journal of Applied Probability, 32(2).

Geske, R. (1979). The valuation of compound options. Journal of Financial Economics, 7(1).

Hull, J. C. (2017). Options, futures, and other derivatives (10th ed.). Pearson.

Johnson, H. (1987). Options on the maximum or the minimum of several assets. The Journal of Financial and Quantitative Analysis, 22(3).

Longstaff, F. A., & Schwartz, E. S. (2001). Valuing American options by simulation: A simple least-squares approach. The Review of Financial Studies, 14(1).

McDonald, R. L. (2013). Derivatives markets (3rd ed.). Pearson.

Natenberg, S. (1988). Option Volatility & Pricing: Advanced Trading Strategies and Techniques.

Pan, J. (2002). The jump-risk premia implicit in options: Evidence from an integrated time-series study. Journal of Financial Economics, 63(1).

Rubinstein, M. (1985). Nonparametric tests of alternative option pricing models using all reported trades and quotes on the 30 most active CBOE option classes from August 23, 1976, through August 31, 1978. The Journal of Finance, 40(2).

Sinclair, N. A. (2008). Volatility trading. John Wiley & Sons.

Taleb, N. N. (1997). Dynamic hedging: Managing vanilla and exotic options. John Wiley & Sons.

Tompkins, R. G. (2001). Implied volatility surfaces: Uncovering regularities for options on financial futures. The Journal of Futures Markets: Futures, Options, and Other Derivative Products, 21(4).

Whaley, R. E. (1986). Valuation of American call options on dividend-paying stocks: Empirical tests. Journal of Financial Economics, 10(1).

Exclusive Bonuses

Dear Reader,

I am thrilled to present to you an exclusive collection of five bonuses, meticulously crafted to enhance your experience and expertise in options trading. These resources are designed to deepen your understanding, refine your strategies, and elevate your trading performance.

- **Bonus 1 - Trading Strategies: A Concise Guide to Hypothetical Analysis in Options Trading**
  This guide offers a deep dive into the world of hypothetical analysis in options trading. It provides you with step-by-step strategies to evaluate potential trades, helping you understand the nuances and complexities of various market scenarios.

- **Bonus 2 - Finding Your Edge: A Personal Guide to Assessing Your Options Trading Style**
  Tailored to help you discover and refine your unique trading style, this guide encourages self-assessment and introspection. It assists you in identifying your strengths, weaknesses, and preferences in the trading world, enabling you to develop a style that resonates with your trading goals.

- **Bonus 3 - Quick Wins in Options: The Essential Cheat Sheet for Trading Success**
  This cheat sheet is a goldmine of tips and tricks for quick wins in options trading. It's designed to provide you with

concise, actionable strategies that can be easily implemented, offering a fast track to success in your trading endeavors.

- **Bonus 4 - Test Your Trade: The Technical Readiness Quiz for Options Traders**
An interactive quiz that assesses your technical readiness and knowledge in options trading. It's a fun and informative way to gauge your understanding of key concepts and to identify areas where you may need further study or practice.

- **Bonus 5 - Trade and Reflect: The Ultimate Journal Template for Options Traders**
This journal template is an invaluable tool for tracking your trades, reflecting on your decisions, and planning future strategies. It helps you document your trading journey, allowing for better analysis, learning, and growth as a trader.

How to Access Your Bonuses:

Scan the QR Code Below: Simply use your phone's camera or a QR code reader to scan the code, and you'll be instantly directed to the bonus content.

Visit the Link: Alternatively, you can access these invaluable resources by visiting this link https://bit.ly/Gastrell-OT (Attention: The link is case-sensitive. Enter the link exactly as it is, with the correct uppercase and lowercase letters. Otherwise, the link will not work properly)

These bonuses are designed to provide you with comprehensive, practical tools and insights that are essential for thriving in the dynamic world of options trading. I am confident that they will be an invaluable part of your trading journey.

Thank you for choosing to embark on this path of financial growth and mastery with us.

Warm regards,

Harry Gastrell